DELIVERED
from
EVIL

RICK JOYNER

DELIVERED
from
EVIL

Preparing for the Age to Come

Destiny Image₀ Publishers, Inc.
P.O. Box 310
Shippensburg, PA 17257-0310

*"Speaking to the Purposes of God for This Generation
and for the Generations to Come"*

ISBN 0-7684-2235-3

For Worldwide Distribution
Printed in the U.S.A.

This book and all other Destiny Image, Revival Press, MercyPlace, Fresh Bread, Destiny Image Fiction, and Treasure House books are available at Christian bookstores and distributors worldwide.

1 2 3 4 5 6 7 8 9 10 / 09 08 07 06 05 04

For a U.S. bookstore nearest you, call
1-800-722-6774.

For more information on foreign distributors, call
717-532-3040.

Or reach us on the Internet:
www.destinyimage.com

Table of Contents

PART 1:
A Deadly Disguise

PART 2:

The Stronghold of Confusion

PART 3:

The End of the Beginning

Preface

This is the third book in a series on spiritual warfare that began with *Breaking the Power of Evil*, and continued with *Overcoming Evil in the Last Days*. These are each expanded and compiled versions of a series of booklets that I wrote on spiritual strongholds, which have continued for years to be very popular.

Even though these books were written to each stand alone, and therefore can be read out of sequence and easily understood, the most basic principles of spiritual warfare are included in the first book of the series. I do include a little review of these principles in the second and third books, but for someone to whom spiritual warfare is new I would recommend reading *Breaking the Power of Evil* before the other two. It not only includes the basic principles of spiritual warfare, but also the basic principles of spiritual authority. It is in this volume that we also address how to break the spirit of poverty, which is possibly the most effective weapon of the enemy of our souls to keep us from our purpose in God.

In *Overcoming Evil in the Last Days* we study some of the most powerful strongholds of our times, including racism, witchcraft, and the religious spirit. In this book we also examine the strategy of the accuser, which is to keep Christians fighting among themselves so that they cannot unite against the strongholds of the devil to bring them down.

In all of these we take a step-by-step approach to unraveling and bringing down these strongholds using the truth of the Scriptures. In this book, *Delivered From Evil*, we will address several of the most powerful strongholds of our time: fear, confusion, and lawlessness, or rebellion.

Of course, there are other spiritual strongholds that keep people in bondage, such as lust, addictions, bitterness, and a host of others. Some of these are addressed in a small measure in these books, but they are certainly worthy of much deeper studies. The reason that I chose the specific strongholds that are addressed in these books is because I (and fellow ministers) have been given insight into them and have had a certain degree of success in seeing people set free from them. We have also found that these are roots that are used to feed the other strongholds, and once they are broken, victory seems much easier over the others.

Even though the Lord Jesus Himself devoted nearly one third of His ministry and teaching to spiritual warfare, as did the first century apostles and writers of the New Testament, spiritual warfare alone is not our purpose nor the whole answer to our victory over evil. King David is probably the greatest warrior in Scripture. He was the first leader of Israel to conquer all of the land that the Lord had promised to His people. He was also probably the greatest worshiper in Scripture. These two, worship and warfare, go together. It does seem that in Scripture, and in our experience, a person cannot really be good at one of these without being good at the other also. This is why we are told in Psalm 149:5-6:

> *Let the godly ones exult in glory; let them sing for joy on their beds. Let the high praises of God be in their mouth, and a two-edged sword in their hand.*

Therefore we do "exult in glory," keeping our attention and devotion to the glory of the Lord. We want to ever be focused on thanking and worshiping Him, which we cannot help but do when we see His glory. Yet, even in worship we do not take off our armor, and we keep the sword in our hand and will be skilled in using it when needed.

Even though one third of the angels may have fallen, two thirds did not. That means that the good angels outnumber the bad—two to one. However, even if they had all fallen, God would still outnumber them. God will win. Evil will ultimately be completely and forever vanquished. The victory is sure.

Certainly the Lord Jesus could have vanquished all evil on the earth immediately after His resurrection. He had paid the price, and He has the authority and power. Yet, He did not do this for our sake. How is this going to be for our sake?

The bride of the first Adam lived in a perfect world and yet chose evil over obedience, leading her husband to disobedience as well. From that time on, satan has had a boast before God. His boast is that even God's crowning creation, man, who was created to have a special and intimate relationship with God, loves his (the devil's) ways more than God's. Before the end of this age the bride of the "last Adam," the Church, will live in the most difficult of times, and against the whole onslaught of evil, she will choose to obey.

Before the end of this age there will be a Church that will be an eternal witness that righteousness prevails over wickedness, and truth will ultimately defeat every lie. This will be even a witness to principalities and powers that good is stronger than evil.

However, the Church will not prevail in this way just because we have learned some better techniques of spiritual warfare and have therefore outsmarted the devil. We will never outsmart the devil. He has been around for thousands of years, has the experience of zillions of cases, and he was smarter than us in the first place. This is not just about strategy—it is about heart. The most powerful weapon that we have is not the sword in our hand, it is the love in our heart.

Truth is important. It is the truth that sets us free. It is the light that casts out darkness. Even so, we will not use the divinely powerful weapons that we have been given rightly if we do not have His love in our hearts. It is not just *having* the truth, but *loving* the truth, that will bring us the victory. It will not just be duty that enables us to go forth setting the captives free; it will be our love for them that keeps us going. Above all, it will be our love for God that keeps us on the path of life, and through which the life will flow through us that overcomes death, the ultimate enemy to be overcome.

Therefore our pursuit must always be far more devoted to knowing God and loving Him—which will also cause us to love His children—than any other matter, including spiritual warfare. It seems that nothing proves character like conflict, which is why the Lord has let the devil and his hordes continue on until this time. Even so, we do not just fight for what we will attain, or even just for the victory, but we fight for our King and His kingdom.

PART ONE

A DEADLY DISGUISE

《❦1❧》

Flies and Lies

The most effective deceptions are based on partial truths. For this reason the devil rarely tries to completely blind people from the truth, but rather he places a veil over their eyes so that what they see is distorted. In this chapter we are going to address two of these veils that have been especially effective in doing great damage to believers, the Church, and the Church's message to the world.

FLIES AND LIES

One of the most devastating ploys of the devil has been to get Christians to develop theologies and beliefs from wounds, rejections, or failures rather than from the Scriptures. The most tragic mistakes and diabolical deeds done by Christians throughout history were done in response to theologies and beliefs that were developed in this way.

It is for this reason that satan is called *beelzebub*, which means "lord of the flies." In dreams and visions, flies usually represent lies. Flies swarm to wounds just as lies swarm to spiritual wounds. The diaries of soldiers involved in great battles tell of the loud hum over a battlefield created by the flies. In this same way satan leads his minions to spiritual battlefields—such as church splits, moral failures of leadership, or doctrinal wars—to swarm over the wounded and spread his deadly infections.

One of the reasons why priests in the Old Testament could not have scabs was because a scab is an unhealed wound, and an unhealed wound will attract flies and become a breeding ground for disease. Priests had to touch people to do their job, and therefore could infect many people if they were carriers of disease or infection.

The same is true spiritually. How many of our true beliefs, those that affect our actions, are based more on our own experience than on the Scriptures? Every single Christian that I know who is no longer a part of a local church, or who has fallen into a serious deception, has unhealed wounds that the enemy has been able to keep infected. Most are spreading their infections to others.

One famous example of destructive theology that was developed by rejection was Martin Luther's persecution of the Jewish people. Many blame the Nazi persecution of the Jews on Luther's special animosity toward them. Although Christian persecution of the Jewish people actually has much deeper roots, Luther's teachings certainly fueled this persecution and helped to perpetuate it. Luther's abhorrence for the Jewish people can be traced back to the rejection he experienced from the rabbis whom he tried to convert with his Reformation gospel. Because Luther had such spiritual authority and reached so many people, his infection spread to multitudes and was perpetuated for generations to come.

Luther is one of the more famous examples of this principle in Church history. However, the overall effect of little wounds, little rejections, and little failures that have influenced the direction of many small churches and multitudes of individual Christians will probably weigh in the balance as having been even more devastating to Christianity than these big ones. As we are told in Song of Solomon 2:15, "The little foxes...are ruining the vineyards."

DEATH BY PAPER CUTS

A lot of little cuts from a penknife can be just as deadly as one big cut from a large sword. However, because the penknife is not perceived as a great threat, no one ever built a shield for protecting against penknives. Likewise, most churches and individual Christians are neutralized by a lot of little wounds rather than one big one.

Each little wound can be used to darken our perspective a little, just like a thin veil. As they add up they become a major restriction of our vision. This cripples our ability to go forward in our faith. Because of this we are told:

> But we all, with unveiled face, beholding as in a mirror the glory of the Lord, are being transformed into the same image from glory to glory, just as from the Lord, the Spirit (2 Cor. 3:18).

This scripture highlights the truth that we will be changed into what we are beholding. We must behold the glory of the Lord with an "unveiled face" to be changed into His image. If we are beholding His glory through a veil, we will see a distorted image of Him and will therefore be changed into a distorted image of Him. This is why much of the Church is a distorted version of what she is intended to be—her vision has been clouded by many veils.

Discerning that wounds, rejections, and failures are potential means through which the enemy can darken a heart is crucial for all who are going to advance in the purposes of the Lord. Spiritual advancement requires us to grow in faith. Unhealed wounds cause us to grow in doubt. We cannot walk in this world without suffering some wounds, rejections, and failures. We must learn to accept them when they happen as part of the process—get over them and keep on going. We must not allow wounds, rejections, or failures to dictate what we believe or our course in the Lord.

STEPPING STONES OR STUMBLING BLOCKS

When we fail we need to evaluate why. Sometimes the people involved, including ourselves, could be more at fault than the plan itself. Or it could be the wrong place, bad timing, or a host of other factors. Thomas Edison logged one thousand failed experiments before he invented a successful light bulb. He considered every failed experiment important because he gained understanding from them that ultimately led to his most important success. A failure can be a most important stepping stone if we approach it rightly, or stumbling block if we don't.

How many times did the apostle Peter fail in his life? Countless. Yet what made him one of the greatest leaders of the Church was that his failures did not cause him to quit. How many of us could say that we would *not* have quit after the Son of God Himself called us "satan"? Yet Peter's tenacity to continue on even after so many personal failures caused the Son of God to give him the keys to the kingdom, an honor not shared by any of the others.

Death by Idealism

Second only to the theologies and beliefs developed by wounds, rejection, and failures, idealism is one of the most effective enemies of the truth. This deception is usually the result of the exact opposite issues from those we covered in the previous chapter, being rooted more in a lack of experience and the wisdom that comes from it.

Idealism has also proven especially deadly because it is usually rooted in a sincere religious zeal. After all, it is difficult for the devil to stop people who are in pursuit of the truth, yet he knows that he can often accomplish even more destruction by getting behind them and pushing them too far. Religious idealism is the tendency to take things beyond what the Lord has directed.

This contributed to the original fall of man. When the serpent asked Eve if the Lord had told her not to eat the fruit of the Tree of the Knowledge of Good and Evil, she responded that He had said not to eat it "or touch it." The Lord had said nothing about touching it. This tendency to go a little further than directed may seem harmless, but when people add to the word of God it reveals a pride in their life that the enemy can easily exploit. Adding to the word of God can be as destructive as taking away from it. This is why those who were the most zealous for the Lord and His word, the Pharisees, were the greatest enemy of the Word Himself when He walked the earth.

The problem here is not religious zeal. Zeal is something that most believers can use a lot more of. The problem comes when Christians combine this zeal with pride, which results in idealism, and therefore becomes destructive. It is especially deceptive because it has such an appearance of goodness and zeal. However, it is goodness from the Tree of the Knowledge of Good and Evil, and therefore has a deadly fruit. Now let's look at a couple of examples of how this manifests and does its destructive work.

CHURCH IDEALISM

The Church, which is called to represent the Lord on earth, should live by and project the highest standards of morality, integrity, justice, and power, as all of these are basic characteristics of the Lord. Even so, the Church is a work in process. Every believer must grow up into who they are called to be, as must every congregation and movement. Idealism applied to the church can be destructive by requiring standards that a church at its present level of maturity cannot live up to. This not only leads to frustration and discouragement, but can distract us from our very calling.

These too high and too unrealistic standards are almost always motivated by a desire to see and live by the very best, which we should all have. However, it is in its unrealistic application that the destructiveness comes. We should have a vision of the highest and best, but we must learn to resist the enemy's attempts to push us too far, or too fast. Along with our vision of going to the highest we need to have a clear understanding of the next step.

However, the steps that are required for solid spiritual progress are usually too little or too slow-moving to satisfy the impatience that will usually accompany one who is driven by idealism in place of a true vision from the Holy Spirit. We must recognize that a vision from the Holy Spirit will come with the fruit of the Spirit, and impatience is not a fruit of the Spirit. As we are told in James 3:17-18:

> *But the wisdom from above is first pure, then peace-able, gentle, reasonable, full of mercy and good fruits, unwavering, without hypocrisy. And the seed whose fruit is righteousness is sown in peace by those who make peace.*

Patience is a fruit of the Spirit, not impatience. We discern that which is coming from the Lord by the peace that it brings. If it brings impatience, striving, anxiety, etc., it is not from above, and we must not let it dictate our course.

If the Church were today all that she was ever going to be, there are probably few true Christians who could live with the disappointment. It does not take a prophet to discern that the Church in its present state will not survive much longer. We are in need of radical change. However, we do not want change for the sake of change, or out of desperation, but from the leading of the Lord. He is the One who will build His Church, and we want to be changed into the image of what we are called to be—the image of the Lord.

In the end only true New Testament Church life is going to survive. It is therefore crucial that we have a vision of the Church becoming much more than we are now, and we also need to moor our vision to Scripture. We do not just want to have a vision, but we want the Lord's vision. We do not want a vision that falls short of this, or that stretches the biblical testimony with human idealism.

When we have gained authority and influence in the Church through the proper channel, the Lord's endorsement, then we must still convey our vision in a way that imparts a clear understanding of where we are, where we're going, and the steps required to get there. If we do not do this properly those with human idealism will usually seize it and, out of zeal, push it far off course.

VISION BY TEAM

There should be a place in the Church where any member can share what they believe they have received from the Lord as a vision for the Church. However, for the Church to embrace a vision, it needs to be tempered by a proper biblical process. For almost any vision to be properly conveyed it does need to come through the team that the Lord has established for the equipping and preparation of His Church, the five equipping ministries listed in Ephesians 4.

Prophets need teachers to make their visions understandable and pastors to make them practical. We need apostolic authority to implement them and evangelistic zeal to help motivate those who are called to do the work of this ministry. We will never have true New Testament Church life until the ministries in the Church learn to work together as the team that they are called to be. This will require humility on the part of all members to help destroy the roots of human idealism that is an enemy of true vision.

A VISION GONE AWRY

Now I want to share an example of how idealism can be destructive in the Church. When I was a relatively new believer, I read a book about the early Church that supposedly represented what true New Testament Church life was supposed to be. It was well written, gripping in its narrative, and wonderful for imparting vision for something more than Church life is presently. However, this book did have a subtle attitude sown throughout it that any church that did not meet up to the standards that were projected in it was not a true New Testament church, and should therefore be discarded. This set off a wave of destruction in the Church, without leaving anything concrete behind to take the place of what was destroyed.

The vision in this book was good, but it left out the practical steps toward accomplishing it. The author's intention was to sow vision, and since the book was very large as it was, there simply was not room to get practical. Sowing vision is not wrong, but we need to have the wisdom to know that before we start out on a journey in response to a vision we need some practical understanding of how to get there.

As this book became more widely read, I watched as many new Christians who were the most zealous for the Lord became discouraged with the church as it was. Then they became critical and scorned any fellowship that did not meet up to their new standards of church life. Then they left their churches and fellowships to pursue this new ideal. Just within my own little circle at the time I witnessed several promising churches and new fellowships actually shut down because of this book. I also watched many of these new believers who had become so idealistic fall away.

Now was this the fault of the book or just the immature and overly zealous people who read it? I have received reports of some of my own books being used in this same way, though it was certainly not what I intended. We have even more examples of the Bible being used in this same way! Does this mean that we should warn people not to read the Bible? That's what the Church in the Middle Ages did, which created even more apostasy, more perversion, and more destruction to the whole Church when the Bible was rediscovered.

My point is that there are changes in the Church that are needed, and both the truth and the times will demand it, but we must be sure that we are following the Lord and not just becoming idealistic reactionaries. Along with our long-term vision of the top of the mountain, we need to see the next practical and safe step up the mountain.

A Vision That Works

After reading the aforementioned book on the early Church, and being both encouraged by it and discouraged by the results I saw, I then read *Church on the Way* by Jack

Hayford. This was a great book, but compared to the one I had read on the early Church, it seemed so mild that it seemed boring. However, there was something very remarkable and powerful about this book: The church it talked about existed! You could go out there and see it, and what you found had not been exaggerated.

It was also refreshing to read a book like this where the author was not constantly telling you how your church should be just like his. Hayford was just sharing encouraging insights that he thought could help others from his own experience in church life.

Now please bear with me while I give a little disclaimer about my home church, MorningStar Fellowship Church. In almost every service, we have people visiting us from around the world. We have never counted the countries they have come from, but they have certainly represented over one hundred nations, and maybe many more. This is encouraging in one way, but in another it is very sad. Let me explain.

I have had Christian leaders with significant influence throughout the Body of Christ, who travel extensively throughout the Body of Christ, tell us that we are the only church they have found that has successfully incorporated the prophetic ministry into the life of the local church. Others have said we were the only church they have visited that has a true team ministry leading the church. I, too, travel quite extensively, and I have to admit that I do not know of another church anywhere that has either of these to the degree that we do. I am not boasting about this, but rather lamenting.

Also, this does not mean that such churches do not exist just because I have not seen them. I may have traveled quite extensively, but I have not been everywhere. Even so, the reason why this is such a grave concern is because our church is really at a low level in both of these areas—incorporating the prophetic ministry into the life of the church, and team ministry. If we are leaders in these areas, then there exists an incredibly low state of New Testament Church life today.

I recently asked the Lord how far we had come, and His reply was that we were now at about 15 percent of the way to being the church He has called us to be. Believe it or not, this was a great encouragement to me! I had no idea we had gotten that far! The Lord also said that He was very pleased with this progress we had made, but we also need to understand how far there is yet to go.

To be straightforward, I am not at all convinced that I will be able to lead our church to the fulfillment of its purpose. I want to, but I am not certain that I have what it will take to do this. This is not false humility, nor a complaint. I see it as a relay race, and I want to run as far as I can and as fast as I can, and then turn the baton over to the next person to run in as good a shape as possible. My goal is simply to be obedient, to do the Lord's will, and to hear those wonderful words on that great day, "Well done, good and faithful servant." Therefore I do a lot with the future generation in mind, wanting to give to them a church that is in as good a shape as possible so that I can rejoice with them as a member of that "great company of witnesses."

On the other hand, I pray often for a vision of the finished work and labor to see the work finished if possible. Therefore I am constantly evaluating where and how to take more ground. I do think we have gained more ground in some areas than most have at this time, and I know other churches that have taken much more ground in areas that we are still very weak in. These we are always seeking to find for interchange and for finding ways to help each other.

We all prophesy in part, see in part, and know in part. Even if we have the biggest part in one area we are still only a little part of the whole. Our goal is to keep taking ground in the areas that we have been able to, and not give up on the areas that we have not been very good at (and there are plenty of those).

Like most churches, we now have a core of some wonderful, faithful people who have been with us for a long time, and we feel that most of them will be with us until the end. We have others who are only supposed to be with us for a short time, to get something that they need from us, and often to give us something that we need.

We also have a continual swirl of people around who are disgruntled and disappointed in us because we did not measure up to their expectations. Some of these are simply a drag to be around, while others go on to be genuine stumbling blocks. When I inquired of the Lord about those who were causing problems He said simply that we would have them with us always, just as He did. In fact, He said that we could never become what we were called to be without them. They supply many of the tests and trials that help us to grow. He said that we should never want to be one of them, but they were allowed for our perfecting, and even the perfect church would have them, just as the perfect ministry would, just as He did. Since we are so far from the perfect church, or the perfect ministry, how much more should we expect from them?

There can be a tendency when you are preaching to have almost the entire congregation on the edge of their seats, cheering you on, but you will inevitably be tempted to focus on the one person who is sleeping, or the one who seems to be rejecting what you are saying. Then you can start to turn your whole message toward them instead of feeding the 90 percent who really are hungry and open for what you have to say. I have watched many preachers and worship leaders stumble in this.

My point is that we cannot allow the idealistic and disgruntled to affect what we are doing. They are there to help us, but not in the way that they want to do it. They are messengers from the devil that the Lord allowed him to send for our sake. However, just as the Lord used the nations around Israel to discipline His people, and then would judge those nations for their presumption, we must always be careful how we relate to the church.

Now I confess that sometimes (too often) I get really irritated with my wife or children and raise my voice at them. Usually I do not even realize that I am raising my voice, but just think I am "being intense." However, if someone else did this to my wife or my children, they would have a serious problem with me. I think the Lord feels the same way about His wife and children.

The Lord told me to speak to His wife like I would to a queen. She is a queen—and more than a queen, she is the bride of the King of kings! She needs a lot of help from those who can tell her when she is making a mistake, but let us do it with the utmost respect and deference. Enough said?

THE IMMATURE AND UNSTABLE

Peter wrote that immature and unstable people were distorting Paul's teachings, and by this bringing destruction upon themselves (see 2 Pet. 3:16). This is not the fault of Paul's teachings, the Bible, or some of the other books and teachings that are thus misused. However, in the book that I previously referred to, I do think that it caused so much turmoil because of the idealism and critical spirit that was sown throughout it. This will always agitate the rebellious and idealistic, but just because the rebellious and idealistic use something to foment their ways does not necessarily mean that there is a problem with what they are using.

That being said, even if we have a true vision given to us from above, we must be careful how we project it. The way that we convey a vision is usually purified by the process that goes with walking out the vision. Walking out a vision will quickly sift out human idealism from the truth. That is why we need to examine the fruit of a projected vision. If there is not fruit, or someone just has a vision but has not walked it out, it is likely to do more damage than good even if it is a vision from above. That is what Paul meant when he said that he would not boast in anything except what the Lord had accomplished through him.

On the book I discussed above about the early Church, when I did a little research on the author I found out that he had neither raised up such a church as he was projecting, or been a part of one either. He was gathering a little band around him who had his same vision, and they set about to pursue it, which was the right thing to do, but they too fell far short of their goal. To date, nearly 30 years later, this vision still has not been realized anywhere on earth that I know of. However, that does not mean that we should give up on it, but we do need to acknowledge that we are still lacking some practical understanding, and maybe even the commission of the Lord in this matter.

Of the people that I have kept up with who left their churches and fellowships to pursue this vision, I do not know of one who is in effective ministry today. Most are even more trapped in this delusion because it is now combined with bitterness and disappointment—three cords that are not easily broken.

I am sure that it was never the author's intent to cause such devastation in the Church, but the damage was still done. I believe there is much merit to his vision of what true New Testament church life should be like, but the problem was in the way that it was presented. It encouraged people to try to leap straight from the bottom of the mountain to the top without receiving the necessary wisdom and maturity that comes from the climb itself.

Again, it is important to project a vision for going higher, but when that vision includes condemnation for what does not presently meet the standard, we should recognize a sure sign that something is wrong. If you want to confirm that something is awry, visit the author or teacher of such a vision and see if their church lives up to the standard that is projected.

It is wrong to tear down something unless we have something built to take its place. If we are going to knock the foundation out from under people, we had better have one that they can stand on that is more than just a vision. Rarely are those who are the true builders concerned about tearing down what is. As the old proverb states, "Any jackass can kick a barn down, but it takes a skillful carpenter to build one."

True builders are too busy building to tear down other people's works. When the true has come, that which is false will collapse on its own. Human idealism that is the enemy of true revelation, and the enemy of the true work of God, will almost always be easily distinguished by its critical, judgmental spirit. This is the spirit of the accuser, not the true friend of the Bridegroom.

Regardless of what we may think of the Church in its present condition, we should always remember that she is the bride of Christ. She may be far from what she is called to be at this time, but she is still the queen. We must treat her with all of the dignity and respect that the queen deserves, especially the queen who is wife of the King of kings. It is sometimes right to bring prophetic correction to even the queen, but I would never want to do it without knowing that I was sent by the King, and even then I would do it with the utmost respect and dignity that the queen deserves.

IDEALISM THAT DESTROYS MARRIAGES

Have you ever wondered why so many of the seemingly most effective teachers, counselors, and authors who speak about what a glorious Christian marriage is supposed to be like end up in divorce themselves? Just as human idealism has been one of the greatest enemies of the emerging of the glorious Church, human idealism can also be found at the root of the most destructive forces tearing apart marriages and families.

Pursuing God's ideal for marriage is certainly one of the most important and noble devotions that we can have. Our success in leading our family is a foundation for any other true success that we can have in our life. The importance of this is the reason why the marriage relationship is under one of the most determined onslaughts of the devil at this time. However, the nature of the devil's most effective strategy against marriage has been comprehended by very few. It is *human idealism of what marriage should be like.*

There are many great books on marriage that every couple should read. They can help to get your marriage off on a much stronger foundation, or they can help you get your relationship back on track if you have run into problems. However, there are also books on marriage that are rooted more in human idealism that can be very destructive to a marriage. These project ideals that no marriage can live up to. The results of these have been multitudes of men and women who are discouraged or frustrated because their relationship, and their spouses, do not live up to the expectations created by this idealism.

I have known many with great marriages, but I have never known anyone with a perfect marriage. I have witnessed many who would probably at least have a good marriage, and maybe even a great one, who are instead divorced because of the discouragement and frustration created by unrealistic ideals and expectations sown in them.

We can protest that Philippians 4:13 states that "I can do all things through Him who strengthens me," so certainly we can become the husband or wife that we are called to be. That is true, but the Lord will strengthen us to become what He has called us to be, not what human idealism tries to impose on us.

UNDERSTANDING LOVE

The Lord wants every husband to love his wife just as Christ loves the Church. Without question the Lord loves His bride more than we can humanly perceive, or have the capacity to love ourselves. He is therefore not calling men to love their wives as much as He loves His Church, but in the same way. He laid down His life for His bride, and we are called to lay down our lives for our wives as well. However, the modern, human ideals of this love and the way that the Lord loves His Church are often very different.

For example, have you ever considered the persecution, attacks by the devil, and other problems that the Lord allows His bride to suffer? Would you purposely allow such things to come upon your spouse? Now, some of you probably too energetically said, "Yes!" Even so, realistically it is natural for us to try to protect our families from attacks and trials. However, the Lord actually allows them for the good of His bride. It is sometimes hard to understand this kind of love, but it is a higher love, and one that human idealism cannot understand.

Let's consider another thing about our perfect husband, the Lord Jesus. Have you considered that He said He was coming "quickly" nearly 2,000 years ago? Since He has such a different interpretation of "quickly" than we do, that probably means that He is not going to show up for dinner when we want or expect Him to. He obviously sets His own schedule and may not even feel inclined to tell us about it. Basically, He is going to be the Lord in this relationship!

I have never been in a marriage counseling session when the woman spoke first that she did not complain that she was not being loved by her husband as Christ loves the Church. I have always wondered, and usually ask, if they have really thought about the way that the Lord loves His Church. Neither have I ever seen a wife making such a complaint who was submitting to her husband "as unto the Lord" as the same text demands.

If the man speaks first it will likewise be to hold up how his wife will not submit to him the way the Scriptures demand, but neither is he loving his wife the way they demand. Most couples will confess that they are falling short on their part, and agree to start doing their part as soon as their spouse does, which usually results in a stalemate.

Coach Bill McCartney (founder of Promise Keepers) shared at one of our recent conferences that his wife just told him that he had finally become the husband that she had dreamed of having. The important revelation here is that Coach is in his 60s, and they have been married for about 40 years. It took that long for him to become the husband she was looking for. How many brides would have entered into a marriage if they knew it was going to take that long for their husband to be what they were hoping for? How many husbands would get married if they knew it would take that long for their wives to become what they were called to be?

I have never read a book on marriage that projected such a long-term vision of this relationship becoming what it is called to be, but I think such a book would be much more realistic. Most of us leap into our marriage with fairy tale ideals and are shocked by how far from these ideals reality really is. We have been tricked! God gave us marriage as one of the primary ways that He works on us to fashion us into His image. As we mature we start to understand that the Lord is not really trying to change us—He's trying to kill us! That means the cross!

True spiritual change requires a death, and then a resurrection. That is why the Lord said in Matthew 16:25, "For whoever wishes to save his life will lose it; but whoever loses his life for My sake will find it." This is true in our relationship to the Church, our spouse, and every other relationship we are called to have.

(C3D)

High Standards
With Wisdom

I will continue a bit with the theme of marriage because it is the model for our relationship to the Lord. In truth, as imperfect and selfish as we are, and the way marriage is especially suited to flushing out these flaws, even if it takes 40 years to do it, the quest for a glorious marriage can be one of the most noble, exciting, and fulfilling parts of our life on this earth. Throw into the mixture the raising of children and it gets even harder, and better. Marriage is the ultimate human relationship, and we must seize it as the wonderful opportunity that it is to grow into who God has called us to be.

Marriages can become what they are supposed to be much faster than is typical, but that is always determined by our own willingness to die to self. All human relationships are hard. Remember that when there were just two brothers on the entire earth one of them basically said, "This place isn't big enough for the both of us!"

Because men and women were created with so many basic differences, marriage can be the most difficult relationship of all, which also gives it the potential to be the most fulfilling of all. That should always be our goal, and it is not idealism.

TAKE ONE STEP

If your marriage is in troubled waters, or at an impasse, there is one step that can break the log jam and begin turning it around. We are told in First Peter 4:8 that "...love covers a multitude of sins." Therefore if we want to grow in love we need to seize every opportunity to cover transgressions. Consider the things that irritate you the most about your spouse as your great opportunity to grow in love by overlooking them.

Some marriage books encourage you to write down the things you like the most about your spouse, as well as the things you don't like about them. Then, for the sake of communication, you share your lists with each other. This may be helpful, but I encourage you to first take the one thing that irritates you the very most about your spouse and resolve not to share it with them. Instead, use it as your opportunity to grow in love for them by covering it or overlooking it. You can also try this in any other relationships that you have.

This can be hard to do at first, but you will be amazed at how you will start to appreciate every time your spouse does the thing that irritates you—because you start to count the trials as joy knowing how they are helping you to grow in the one characteristic that can help us the most in life. Without love, everything that we do, even for the Lord, can end up being useless, as we are told in First Corinthians 13.

Another benefit of using another person's faults as a way to grow in love is that it often releases that person to change. Unrighteous judgments (which can be accurate judgments but given in the wrong spirit) can yoke people and make it much harder for them to change. When we are growing in love, instead of criticism and frustration, we are much more likely to give words of encouragement that will help people instead of keeping them in bondage.

Some of the greatest pressures that can come to a marriage will be from idealism that we direct at ourselves. Idealism is usually rooted in a truth, but as we all fall short of the glory, idealism is like the Law that may accurately point out all of our problems, but does not empower us to overcome them. Instead, idealism will have us trying to overcome a hundred different issues at once, fighting battles on far too many fronts, and wearing us out so that no progress is being made anywhere.

Idealism can also have us expecting from our spouses (or our churches) certain fulfillment that we can only get from our relationship to God, or in some cases, other friends. No man can ever be all things to his wife, and no wife can ever be all things to her husband. Neither can the church be all things to all people. Whether you can accept it or not, neither can God even be all that we need because He created us to need other people too. That is why the first thing that He said was "not good" was for "man to be alone," and He said this when man obviously had Him.

No relationship will be what it is supposed to be if God is not our first love, but He did create us to need other people as well. Our spouse should be our next love after God, and then our families, but we need even more than this. Healthy social relationships are essential for a healthy, fulfilling, and successful life.

Think of this—the Father had His Son and the Holy Spirit for fellowship, and then all of the angels, and yet He still created man for fellowship. Was this an affront to His love for His Son and the Holy Spirit? Of course not. The creation of man presented even more opportunities for all of them to express their love and devotion for one another.

Because we were created in the image of God, we likewise need relationships on different levels. If we are healthy and walking in truth, we will keep them in their proper perspective, but we will keep them all.

GOD DISQUALIFIED?

Because the marriage relationship is so crucial for the health of mankind in general, there are higher biblical standards for this relationship required of anyone who would be accepted into a place of authority in the church. The Scriptures declare that one had to be the husband of one wife to be in the position of elder or deacon. We cannot dilute the clear directives of Scripture such as this without eroding the very foundation of the church. So does this directive mean that one cannot have been through a divorce to qualify for leadership in the church? It cannot mean this because if that were true then God could not even be an elder in His church.

In Jeremiah 3:8 it states that God gave Israel a certificate of divorce. Was it God's fault that marriage did not work? Certainly not. One can be the most perfect husband, as God definitely was, and things still not work. God does hate divorce, and it should therefore be resisted to the utmost, but there was a point when even He had to go through one. Now I think the Scriptures are clear that He intends to remarry His estranged wife at the end, but presently God is a divorcee.

As stated, marriage is such a crucial foundation—not only for church life but also for the entire social order of man—that it must be held in the highest regard. The biblical standards for leadership and marital relationships must be complied with. However, the Scripture also states that if an unbeliever leaves a relationship then the believer is no longer bound, which can be interpreted as being free to marry again because that is the only way that they could be bound or unbound.

Even so, one of the growing tragedies of our time is how some leaders have left their wives—the women who bore their children and who supported their devotion to ministry so that they could get to the place where they are now—and then they can run off with a secretary and not even miss a Sunday in the pulpit! This kind of behavior is an affront to God, His Word, and His people, and should not be tolerated.

Any church that has become that desensitized to divorce and immorality has obviously departed far from God.

However, if we have a doctrine that would disqualify even God from being in leadership then we need to reexamine our doctrine. This issue simply needs to be viewed on a case-by-case basis or we will continue to lose some of the best potential leaders in the church.

SUMMARY

There are a multitude of other examples of how idealism can distort our perspective of God, ourselves, and others, resulting in a tragic distortion of the Church. This is why we must heed Second Corinthians 11:3:

> But I am afraid that, as the serpent deceived Eve by his craftiness, your minds will be led astray from the simplicity and purity of devotion to Christ.

Our calling in every relationship is basically for us to grow in love. We can grow faster when the relationship is difficult. We must seize each problem in a relationship as an opportunity to grow in love, and therefore to become more like the Lord. This does not mean that we overlook all problems, but when we confront them we always do it in the right spirit, seeking to help the person who has the problem, not just reacting because we are irritated.

In these times when the most basic fabric of civilization, marriage, is being attacked from so many directions, we must increase our devotion to much better and stronger marriages, and ones that do reflect the Lord's relationship to His Church. However, we must not resort to idealism as that will only weaken them in the end.

We do need to have a vision of walking in the highest purposes of God in everything, but we need to have practical wisdom for how we can get there from where we are. Presently, the frustration created by human idealism and people's inability to live up to its demands is probably doing more damage to marriages than anything else.

Of course, destructive idealism manifests itself in many ways other than just the two examples that we have covered here with the Church and marriage. However, if we can start to see it in these two areas, we will start to recognize it in other ways that it seeks to do its destructive work. When we *see* it, we can effectively *resist* it. When we start to resist satan in this way, he will begin to flee from us. Then the light that we walk in will have the power to cast out the darkness, and we will extend the kingdom wherever we go.

≪4≫

The Great Gathering

Basic to understanding the biblical prophecies of our times is the Lord's statement in Matthew 13:39: "The harvest is the end of the age." As He makes clear in His other parables and statements about the end of the age, this harvest is the reaping of everything that has been sown in man, both the good and the evil. Both are coming to full maturity. The righteous will become more righteous, and the wicked more wicked. Therefore, at the end of the age we will have the ultimate battle between good and evil.

It is for this reason that we must put on the full armor that has been given to us by God and learn how to use our divinely powerful weapons effectively. Two of the most powerful weapons that we have been given are love and truth. Therefore, a most basic goal of our life should be to walk in love and truth in all that we do. As we are told in Romans 12:21: "Do not be overcome by evil, but overcome evil with good."

Basically we overcome every evil released on the earth by growing in God's counterpower to it. We overcome the fear being released on the earth by walking in faith. We overcome hatred and wrath by growing in love. We overcome rebellion and lawlessness by growing in obedience and devotion to the Lordship of Jesus. In this way we discern the evil that is growing in the world and overcome it by ourselves growing in God's grace that counters it.

THE WISDOM OF THE HARVEST

Matthew 13:30 gives us an understanding of many of the things that are going on in our own times. In the parable of the wheat and the tares, the Lord Jesus said:

> *Allow both to grow together until the harvest; and in the time of the harvest I will say to the reapers, "First gather up the tares and bind them in bundles to burn them up; but gather the wheat into my barn"* (Matt. 13:30).

In this parable, we can see a miniature history of the world. The Lord created the earth perfect for His children to grow up in, and the devil came along and sowed tares in God's field. The Lord responded to this by telling His servants to let both the wheat and the tares grow up together, or mature together, and at the harvest (which is the end of the age), they will be separated. This separation is going on right now.

THE SEPARATION

Tares actually look like wheat, but are noxious. It is very hard to tell them apart except at the harvest. The reason that they can be distinguished at the harvest is because as the wheat matures it begins to bow over, while the tares remain standing upright. We might say that with increasing maturity the wheat becomes more humble, and the tares become more arrogant.

I have talked to numerous people who have had dreams or visions of a sword coming that cuts off the head of everyone who is not bowing over. I think this is a prophetic picture of what is coming. Those who are bowed over are the humble who are devoted to prayer. Those who are standing upright here are those who do not humble themselves, and those are the tares that will be cut off.

Presently there probably is not a single church, ministry, or any other spiritual field that does not have tares mixed in with the wheat. As maturity comes, the distinctions will become more pronounced, and the separation easier.

As we are told, we can expect the tares to start gathering together into "bundles." It is noteworthy that in the parable the tares are gathered together first. I think that we can see almost everywhere in the world now that those who are prone to evil have been gathering into organizations, groups, and even communities and nations. Presently they are in more unity than the believers who are the "wheat." Even so, we are now in the time when the "wheat," those who are born of the good seed, will be gathered together, coming into an unprecedented unity.

Because of this unifying of the evil in one group and the righteous in another, we are told in Second Corinthians 6:14:

> *Do not be bound together with unbelievers; for what partnership have righteousness and lawlessness, or what fellowship has light with darkness?*

The Lord does not want us to go out of the world or He would have already taken us out of it. There are relationships that we need and should have with unbelievers in order to be a witness to them. However, we do need to refrain from covenant relationships with unbelievers. That is what it means to be "bound together." Those who are bound together with unbelievers are going to be increasingly torn between one camp or the other, and at some point, trying to live in both worlds will no longer be possible.

We must also be aware of the fact that unifying, for either good or evil, does increase power. As in the parable of the wheat and tares, the evil is gathered into bundles first, and as stated, evil has in fact been unifying more and faster than the Church until now. This is why evil has seemed more powerful and has been advancing far more than the Kingdom in many places. Even so, we are now coming to the time when the wheat will start gathering together, coming into unity, and therefore growing in power. The tide of evil will then be turned, which is already happening in many places.

The main point that I wanted to make in this chapter is that we are going to begin witnessing the gathering together of both the tares and the wheat as we proceed toward the end of this age. The evil will take care of itself, but we must apply ourselves to joining together with other members of the Body of Christ.

THE MAIN THING

One of my favorite quotes is from a man named Peter Lord, who said: "The main thing is to keep the main thing the main thing." Many people do get distracted from the River of Life by a little tributary that feeds it. This leads to the overemphasis of certain teachings, which leads to extremes as well as to the worst deception of all: the pursuit of a doctrine in place of the Lord Himself.

It is also true that some have fallen into worshiping the temple of the Lord, the Church, in place of the Lord of the temple. Even so, the temple is the place where the Lord has prescribed that we worship Him. I say this because it has been estimated that somewhere between 75 percent and 90 percent of those who claim to be Christians do not attend church. This will soon become a tragedy for those in this category.

The Church is not the Kingdom, though it is certainly a part of it, and will be the primary vehicle through which the Kingdom comes. Even so, His Kingdom is far bigger than the Church, and the Church needs to understand all that He is doing because we are called to be His instruments through which does His work on the earth.

Keeping in mind that the main thing is to know the Lord and abide in Him, the main thing that the Lord is doing in the earth is building His Church. If we do not see what He is doing in the Church, we will never be able to understand the other prophecies concerning these times. Even worse, if we are not taking our place in what He is doing in the Church, we will never be in His will.

It is true that you can be joined to the Body in many ways without being properly joined to the Head, but the reverse is not true. You can never be properly joined to the Head unless you are also joined to His Body. We cannot understand what the Lord is doing today without understanding what He is doing in the Church, and we cannot be a part of what He is doing today without being rightly joined to His Church.

For this reason the exhortation of First Corinthians 11:24-30 is crucial if we are going to be a part of God's purposes in the earth, and as the text warns, even survive long on the earth:

> *And when He had given thanks, He broke it and said, "This is My body, which is for you; do this in remembrance of Me." In the same way He took the cup also after supper, saying, "This cup is the new covenant in My blood; do this, as often as you drink it, in remembrance of Me." For as often as you eat this bread and drink the cup, you proclaim the Lord's death until He comes. Therefore whoever eats the bread or drinks the cup of the Lord in an unworthy manner, shall be guilty of the body and the blood of the Lord. But a man must examine himself, and in so doing he is to eat of the bread and drink of the cup. For he who eats and drinks, eats and drinks judgment to himself if he does not judge the body rightly. For this reason many among you are weak and sick, and a number sleep.*

We often quote this when taking communion, but this is not just about the elements of bread and wine, but the truth that these elements represent. All biblical rituals are given to us to represent important truths that should continually be brought to our remembrance. The condemnation in the verses above does not come from refraining to partake of (or participate in) a ritual, but by partaking of the ritual in an unworthy manner, not recognizing the reality that it represents in our life. The transgression that causes the weakness, sickness, and death is to "not judge the body rightly." This remains the main cause of weakness, sickness, and premature death among Christians today.

Again, this is not about the ritual. You can eat all of the bread and drink all of the wine in the county and not have communion. Communion is a symbolic ritual that is intended to convey a profound truth that we must have in our life. The judgment comes when we try to substitute the ritual for the reality that it represents. We will be weak, or sick, and progressing toward death, to the degree that we do not have communion with the Lord and His Body.

In the times that are coming, if we are not rightly joined to the Lord's Body we will be joined to the body of antichrist. It does not matter how much truth we *know*, it is the truth that we are *living* that will determine where we stand.

If you do not have a growing relationship with a church body, you are going to end up in that category—unless you make a radical change in your life now. This change that is needed is to get in a local church body. It is clear in the Scripture that if we do not have this relationship, then we will not discern truth or have His life flowing through us. One example of this is in First John 1:7:

> *If we walk in the Light as He Himself is in the Light, we have fellowship with one another, and the blood of Jesus His Son cleanses us from all sin.*

The word translated "fellowship" in this text is the Greek *koinonia*, which is much more than a handshake with each other on Sunday morning. This represents a joining together to the degree that the blood, or life, of Christ flows from one member to the other.

If you are no longer in a strong church fellowship because you were hurt or disappointed, it is time to be a Christian and forgive, get over it quickly, and get back into fellowship with a strong body of believers. Your life literally depends on it.

I personally doubt that anyone has ever been in any relationship with anyone else where he or she has not suffered some hurt and disappointment. True Christianity is a life founded on forgiveness. Who was hurt more, or rejected more, than Jesus by the very ones He came to save? This is why He told us to take up our crosses daily. We are going to have to die to ourselves somehow every day if we are going to follow Him. If we are not willing to do this, as He Himself said, we are not really following Him.

«5»

The Ultimate Purpose

The most basic purpose of God on the earth is redemption and restoration. If you take the first three chapters of the Bible, and the last three, you have a complete story. Everything between those six chapters deals with one basic subject: the redemption and restoration of man, and the domain that had been given to man, from the fall.

In the apostle Peter's second sermon he made a very important statement about the Lord's return, saying "whom heaven must receive until the period of restoration of all things about which God spoke by the mouth of His holy prophets from ancient time" (Acts 3:21). The "all things" that will be restored is, of course, all that was lost after the fall. There will be a complete restoration of man and all that was under his domain that has likewise been subject to the consequences of the fall. This period of restoration that Peter is talking about here is the reign of Christ on the earth, which we are coming to.

Of course, the Church is called to reign with Him during this period. After the Lord was crucified and raised again the Church became the ultimate vehicle for this ultimate purpose on the earth. This whole age has actually been "training for reigning" for those who are called to be members of His household. The purpose of this reign is restoration. Restoration is therefore one of the most important things that we learn.

The Church has done a fairly good job of preaching redemption, which of course is the first step in our restoration, but there has rarely been a vision and understanding imparted of how, once we are redeemed, we must be restored. This is, of course, clear in the Scriptures, and there are some congregations that do have a great message and an effective ministry in restoration, but overall there is a very important mandate that must be recovered and restored to the Church, so that the Church can be the vehicle that it is called to be in "the restoration of all things."

The first, and most important, thing that was lost by the fall was the intimate fellowship that man had with God. The main purpose of redemption and restoration is to restore that relationship. If there is any way that we can determine the degree to which redemption and restoration has truly worked in our life, it would be by how close to God we have become.

The second most basic thing that was lost by the fall was the depth and quality of the fellowship that man was to have with his fellow man. Remember, the very first thing that God said that was not good was for man to be alone, or loneliness. This was said when man had God, so we can conclude that man was created to need more than just his fellowship with God—he also needed fellowship with other people. He created us to be social beings.

However, when there were just two brothers on the earth they could not get along. One of them basically said, "This world is not big enough for the both of us!" He then killed his brother. People have a hard time getting along. Marriage is one of the greatest things God ever created, and it is also one of the most difficult. It was meant to bless us, and to kill us! Seriously, for a marriage to survive, both husband and wife are required to lay down their lives, their selfishness, and learn to love.

Likewise, the Church is called to be the most wonderful, full of glory and power, united, loving, social entity ever created upon the earth. Before the end of this age, the Church will become all that it was created to be. The very process of growing up into this mighty temple of the Lord will transform us into His image. If we are not willing to submit to the process, we will never be like Him, and therefore we will never do His will.

When the Church really becomes what it is called to be, the whole world will yearn to be a part of such a fellowship. Even though the Church may seem in many ways to be as far from what it is called to be as it ever has been, this will change, and quickly. We really are approaching the end of this age, and we can be sure that before the end comes, the bride of Christ will be all that she was created to be, and she will be a bride worthy of her King. So what will happen will happen fast.

There is a new breed of leadership arising in the Church: shepherds who treat the sheep with all of the care, dignity, and respect that the sons and daughters of the King deserve. They will come with a heart for restoration that is like the Lord's own heart, which they will have developed from the suffering, and enduring, of ministering to those who were so far from what they were called to be—shepherds who did not give up, but persevered until the changes came. These will be overcomers. For this reason, the more difficult the place in which we are presently called to serve, the greater the opportunity to take on the Lord's heart, which is for restoration.

The leaders who are coming will not look at a single congregation of Christians—regardless of what condition it is in—and want to abandon it. Just as the Lord looked down upon the depraved condition of the earth and did not abandon us, but laid down His life to redeem us and restore us, His ministries at the end will have the same heart. They will want to see all restored and become what they were created to be just as the Lord has in His heart the desire for the whole world to be restored and become all that He created it to be.

We will not be joined to the purposes of the Lord without having this heart for restoration. We will not have His heart if we have a tendency to quit on His people. Actually, the worse the condition that a church is in now, the greater the glory will be when it is restored. This is why the Lord promised Zerubbabel that the glory of the latter house would actually be greater than the former, even though it was obvious to all that the latter house was inferior to the former one. The house is not the main point, but rather the glory that is revealed in it.

At the time God told Zerubbabel this, the temple of the Lord was but a huge mountain of rubble. The Lord promised him that this mountain would be made a plain before him, and then exhorted him not to despise the day of small things (see Zech. 4:7-10). Those who are faithful in the little things will be the ones made rulers over the greater ones.

Note that the mountain of stones that Zerubbabel stood before, which had been the former temple and needed to be used to build the second one, were all "burnt stones." If we have not yet been "burned" in our relationship to the church, we probably are not qualified to be used in the most glorious restored temple. That is part of the process. We need to get over it and get back into the ultimate battle on this earth—the battle for God's purposes—the restoration of the earth which will begin with His temple, the Church.

Something restored from devastation is a greater witness than something built from the beginning. It is for this reason that for all of eternity the restored earth will be a witness of the nature of God and the power of good to prevail over evil. Therefore, we cannot understand these times, or be a part of the Lord's purposes in them, without a heart for restoration.

For this reason the Books of Haggai, Zechariah, Ezra, and Nehemiah are crucial for our times. These all addressed the difficulties and triumphs of the remnant that returned to their land to rebuild the temple of the Lord and to restore their nation.

Haggai 2:3-9 says:

"Who is left among you who saw this temple in its former glory? And how do you see it now? Does it not seem to you like nothing in comparison? But now take courage, Zerubbabel," declares the Lord, "take courage also, Joshua son of Jehozadak, the high priest, and all you people of the land take courage," declares the Lord, "and work; for I am with you," declares the Lord of hosts. "As for the promise which I made you when you came out of Egypt, My Spirit is abiding in your midst; do not fear!" For thus says the Lord of hosts, "Once more in a little while, I am going to shake the heavens and the earth, the sea also and the dry land. I will shake all the nations; and they will come with the wealth of all nations, and I will fill this house with glory," says the Lord of hosts. "The silver is Mine and the gold is Mine," declares the Lord of hosts. "The latter glory of this house will be greater than the former," says the Lord of hosts, "and in this place I will give peace," declares the Lord of hosts.

If you are not presently in a local church body, find one to join, quickly. If we are growing closer to the Lord, we will also be getting closer to His people. We can count on there being hurts and disappointments, but every one of those is an opportunity for us to become conformed to His nature. As the apostle John warned, we simply cannot love God without also loving His people. If we are truly growing in our love for God we will also be growing in our love for His people.

There are churches that are going into apostasy, and I am not encouraging you to join them, or stay in one that is making a clear departure from godliness or sound biblical truth. The Scripture clearly warns us to depart from such as that. However, being in the right church where we are called to be should take precedence over where we live much more than a job or profession if we are true seekers of God. Our church life is far more important than any profession can be to us.

The Most Basic Evil

The most basic evil is rebellion against God. That is what released all of the death into the world in the first place, and it is basically what will cause all of the death and destruction in our times. The ultimate lesson that all of creation will learn from what comes upon the world at the end is the consequence of thinking that we can do anything without God. Man was created to need God, and we do need Him. We will make a terrible mess out of anything that we do without Him.

The death and destruction that comes upon the world at the end is not so much the result of God hurling His judgments at the world, as it is the consequences of man's own behavior. A basic spiritual principle is stated in Galatians 6:7: "Do not be deceived, God is not mocked; for whatever a man sows, this he will also reap." Everyone will reap what he or she sows. Much of the destruction that comes at the end is simply the consequences of man's own rebellion and determination to live without God.

The ultimate state of rebellion is known as "lawlessness." That basically means "to be without principles or moral code." That is precisely the state that the wicked are coming to. In contrast to this, the righteous will get more righteous. Their integrity, their moral code, will get stronger and stronger—so will their obedience to the Lord.

THE ULTIMATE EVIL PLAN, AND THE ULTIMATE WITNESS

Satan's ultimate purpose is to declare to the entire creation of God that man, the crown jewel of God's creation, loves satan and his ways more than God and His ways. Presently, satan can point to the Church and boast that even Christians love sin more than they love righteousness. However, when a person is obedient to God and resists the overwhelming temptations and pressures of this world to do evil, and instead remains faithful to God and obedient to Him, that person becomes a witness to even principalities and powers in the heavenly realm.

The bride of the first Adam lived in a perfect world, and yet chose to sin. The bride of the "last Adam" (Christ) will live in the most imperfect world, and against all of the power of evil, and in the darkest of times, she will choose to obey. For this reason all of creation will consider her worthy to reign with the King, Jesus.

Therefore, the ultimate test will be to live in obedience and faithfulness to God or fall into the ranks of lawlessness. Because love is the greatest force behind good, only those who truly love God will remain faithful. This is why the Lord stated in Matthew 24:12-13: "Because lawlessness is increased, most people's love will grow cold. But the one who endures to the end, he will be saved."

In Second Corinthians 13:5, Paul said, "Test yourselves to see if you are in the faith; examine yourselves!" Possibly the most basic test of whether we are remaining in the faith is if God truly is our first love. If He is, then our primary goal in life will be to serve Him, please Him, and do His will.

The Lord said that "most" people's love would grow cold, not just some. This should be a most sobering statement for any Christian to contemplate. What will cause our love to grow cold? The Lord tells us in the same verse: Lawlessness.

Therefore, some of the most important questions we can ask are: Are we allowing our moral standards to erode along with the world's? Which way are we headed, toward greater unity and obedience to the Lord, or toward greater disobedience and lawlessness?

I have seen some Christians comfort themselves by saying that those people whose love grows cold are the heathen, but that does not make sense because the heathen do not have a love for God in the first place. One of the things that we can be sure of at the end is that "most" Christians' love will grow cold, and it will be eroded because of lawlessness. Therefore, lawlessness is one of the ultimate tests that we can expect to try our hearts at the end.

We must therefore be vigilant to watch over our hearts. Begin to ask now, what is happening to our love? If it is not getting stronger, it is getting weaker. Is our love for God being eroded by the lawlessness that is increasing? We are told how this happens in Romans 6:19-23:

> *I am speaking in human terms because of the weakness of your flesh.* **For just as you presented your members as slaves to impurity and to lawlessness, resulting in further lawlessness, so now present your members as slaves to righteousness, resulting in sanctification.** *For when you were slaves of sin, you were free in regard to righteousness. Therefore what benefit were you then deriving from the things of which you are now ashamed? For the outcome of those things is death. But now having been freed from sin and enslaved to God, you derive your benefit, resulting in sanctification, and the outcome, eternal life. For the wages of sin is death, but the free gift of God is eternal life in Christ Jesus our Lord.*

Here we see that impurity leads to lawlessness, and when we give ourselves to impurity and lawlessness, the result is further lawlessness. For example, some people have claimed that they have never been unfaithful to their spouse, but are actually addicted to pornography. Did the Lord not say that if a man even looks upon a woman to lust after her, he has committed adultery in his heart? Even if we have not committed the physical act of adultery or forni-cation, the mental or emotional infidelity is impurity that leads to lawlessness.

When we open the door to the lust of the flesh, which is impurity, we open the door wide to lawlessness. When we do this, the first thing that gets eroded is our love for God. Lust is actually the counter-power of true love, and therefore impu-rity makes true love start to grow cold very fast. As Paul exhorts in Galatians 5:16-25:

> But I say, walk by the Spirit, and you will not carry out the desire of the flesh. For the flesh sets its desire against the Spirit, and the Spirit against the flesh; for these are in opposition to one another, so that you may not do the things that you please. But if you are led by the Spirit, you are not under the Law. Now the deeds of the flesh are evident, which are: immorality, impurity, sensual-ity, idolatry, sorcery, enmities, strife, jealousy, outbursts of anger, disputes, dissensions, factions, envying, drunkenness, carousing, and things like these, of which I forewarn you, just as I have forewarned you, that those who practice such things will not inherit the kingdom of God. But the fruit of the Spirit is love, joy, peace, patience, kindness, goodness, faithfulness, gentleness, self-control; against such things there is no law. Now those who belong to Christ Jesus have crucified

the flesh with its passions and desires. If we live by the Spirit, let us also walk by the Spirit.

If we are not growing in the Spirit, which is accomplished at least partly by crucifying the flesh and its evil desires, we are going to be falling to those things that will cause the wrath of God to ultimately come. If our pursuit is just to not do the things that are evil, we will remain weak. What we must do is grow in God's counter-power to these things. As we are told in First John 3:3-4:

And everyone who has this hope fixed on Him purifies himself, just as He is pure. Everyone who practices sin also practices lawlessness; and sin is lawlessness.

The greatest enemy of godliness and the greatest power of destruction that is coming will be released through lawlessness. The following scriptures are some of the Lord's statements about the consequences of giving ourselves to lawlessness:

Many will say to Me on that day, "Lord, Lord, did we not prophesy in Your name, and in Your name cast out demons, and in Your name perform many miracles?" And then I will declare to them, "I never knew you; depart from Me, you who practice lawlessness" (Matt. 7:22-23).

Could it be possible to "practice lawlessness" and still be able to prophesy, cast out demons, and even perform miracles in the Lord's name? Yes. As we are told in Romans 11:29: "The gifts and the calling of God are irrevocable." This means that when the Lord gives something He does not take it back, even if we become unfaithful. All of the ministries and gifts of the Spirit can go on working in our life even if we have given ourselves over to impurity, immorality, or any other form of lawlessness. That is why we should discern His true servants by their fruit, not just their gifts.

In Matthew 13:41-42, the Lord says:

The Son of Man will send forth His angels, and they will gather out of His kingdom all stumbling blocks, and those who commit lawlessness, and will throw them into the furnace of fire; in that place there shall be weeping and gnashing of teeth.

Here we are told that the time is coming when the Lord will gather these stumbling blocks out of His Kingdom, and without question, all who fall to lawlessness will become stumbling blocks. That is the last thing we should ever want to be because He warned in Luke 17:1-2:

It is inevitable that stumbling blocks come, but woe to him through whom they come! It would be better for him if a millstone were hung around his neck and he were thrown into the sea, than that he would cause one of these little ones to stumble.

In Matthew 23:27-28, we are given another important characteristic of lawlessness:

Woe to you, scribes and Pharisees, hypocrites! For you are like whitewashed tombs which on the out-side appear beautiful, but inside they are full of dead men's bones and all uncleanness. So you, too, out-wardly appear righteous to men, but inwardly you are full of hypocrisy and lawlessness.

Sometimes we think of lawlessness as rebellion, the craftiness that is always trying to bend the rules and get away with it, or even anarchy. Here we see that those who were the most given to keeping the law were "full of hypocrisy and lawlessness." Legalism is not the answer to lawlessness—it actually promotes lawlessness. It promotes cleaning up the externals so that we appear righteous before men, but this actually leads to an even deeper corruption of the heart.

There have been many legalistic movements in the Church that have tried to deliver men from lawlessness through legalism, or even the submission to what is, in fact, a control spirit. These things can change the behavior of some, but they can never change the heart, and it is the heart that God looks upon. The only thing that will really change our heart is love. Those who truly love God are devoted to doing that which pleases Him. Anything but love will eventually wither under the onslaught of lawlessness that is now being released in the world.

Therefore, our ultimate goal should be just what Paul said in First Timothy 1:5: "But the goal of our instruction is love from a pure heart and a good conscience and a sincere faith." There are many practical things that we can do to guard our hearts from the onslaught of lawlessness, simple things like obeying rules, regulations, and laws (speed limits, paying taxes, etc.). We should start loving and deeply appreciating these rules, which anyone would do if they just thought for one moment what this world would be like without them.

THE HIGHEST HONOR

If we were told that a king, or the President, was going to come and stay at our home for a week, would we not go home and scrub, clean, organize, and maybe even paint the house? Some would probably even try to buy a new house! My point is that we have someone living within us now who is much greater than any earthly king or president—we have the Holy Spirit of God! How much more should we be trying to keep our house clean and in order for Him?

Carry this thought a little further. If a king or president did come to your house, and he knew that you had received adequate warning of his arrival, yet the house was still a mess and you had not made any attempt to clean it up, would he not be deeply offended? This is basically what Paul was saying in First Corinthians 3:16-17:

Do you not know that you are a temple of God and that the Spirit of God dwells in you? If any man destroys the temple of God, God will destroy him, for the temple of God is holy, and that is what you are.

The time is coming when the Lord will no longer allow His Holy Spirit to be offended by the shoddy way that some keep His temple. If we truly love the Lord, and honor Him, we would do much better in this than we have been doing.

If we will love God, and love one another, we will stand against any evil that comes in the last days. The primary way that we are called to do this is to prepare for Him a temple in which His glory, His light, can be manifested. We are called to live lives that reveal His glory.

PART TWO

THE STRONGHOLD
OF CONFUSION

《Q7Q》

Understanding Confusion

Confusion is one of the most devastating enemies of truth and human achievement. Confusion can cripple the most brilliant, or the most diligent. For this reason, getting free from confusion can make one of the most radical changes in a person's life, turning it from one of defeat and depression into a life of joy, peace, and fruitfulness. Therefore, recognizing and overcoming the spirit of confusion is essential for all who desire to walk in their destiny and accomplish their purpose.

Living with confusion is like being in a thick fog every day. Many become so accustomed to this that they do not even know that they are living in a state of confusion. Like children with poor eyesight who put on glasses for the first time, they are astonished at the world around them when they break out from under this terrible oppression. As Proverbs 4:18 states, "But the path of the righteous is like the light of dawn, that shines brighter and brighter until the full day." Every Christian should live by a light in their life that gets brighter every day. If this is not the case for you, then there is a good possibility that in some way you have departed from the path that you were called to walk, and by this opened the door to confusion.

However, be encouraged because this can be corrected almost as quickly as the child with poor eyesight who puts on a pair of prescription glasses. Just as this child will immediately see the world differently, when you break the power of confusion off of your life, you too will start to see the world clearly. You will immediately begin to live with a new decisiveness, a confidence, and a peace that others will probably see as miraculous. As a Christian you are not called to live in confusion, but to walk in a light that not only makes your own path clear, but also reveals the path of light to others who are walking in darkness. You must not settle for anything less.

I live on a mountain because I like to be in a place of vision. On a clear day I can see mountain ranges that are nearly a hundred miles away. It is especially beautiful when there is fog in the valley and I can look down on a blanket of white below while standing in bright sunshine. That is the way that we are called to live as Christians—in a place of clear vision above the fog and confusion that is in the world.

If you have ever been in a fog as it began to burn away, then you know how it starts by getting brighter as the sun thins the cloud above you. Then, when the shafts of light begin to break through, you know it will not be long before the fog is completely burned away. In a short period of time your perspective can go from seeing only a few feet to a very long way. This is what happens when someone is delivered from confusion in their life—they are amazed at how far they can suddenly begin to see.

THE SONLIGHT OF UNDERSTANDING

The very title of this chapter, "Understanding Confusion," may seem like an oxymoron. However, it is precisely what one must do to defeat confusion—understanding it is the biggest part of the battle to overcome it. Understanding brings light, and light casts out darkness. When you open your shades at night, darkness does not flow into your house, but rather the light flows out into the darkness. This is because light is more powerful than darkness and will always overcome it. So we will begin this study by shining the light of understanding with a basic definition of confusion. Then we will seek to expand this definition, and our understanding, until there is no place left for it to hide in our life.

The dictionary defines *confuse* as "to make mentally uncertain, to jumble." For the purpose of this study we will define confusion as a spiritual or mental stronghold that prevents clear thinking and understanding. Sometimes confusion can have a physical cause, such as chemical imbalances in the body that affect our mental activity and clarity. In such cases, it can usually be overcome with such things as diet and exercise. However, the root of this problem is usually spiritual. It is a very real "living" enemy that has a mind of its own, and a strategy that it is using against us. Just recognizing it as a problem can illuminate its strategy and begin to unravel its web in our life.

Obviously confusion can range in power and degree. It can work to keep us from understanding a single matter clearly, but it can also be so pervasive that it keeps us from understanding almost anything clearly. Even if our state of confusion seems relatively mild, we must resolve not to allow any of it in our life. Once confusion gets a foothold into just one part of our life, it will begin to undermine our faith and our confidence, and eventually it will spill over into other areas of our life. Its goal is the complete disruption of our life. Confusion wants to hinder our progress in everything. If it is not cut off at its root, like a weed it will come back and multiply. This is why our goal must be to understand the roots of confusion and learn to pull it out by its roots so that it cannot come back or spread.

You can be sure that regardless of how tightly confusion has gotten a grip on your life, you can be completely free from it. That is the goal of this book—to help you get completely free of confusion so that in place of the clouds and gloom you will walk every day in increasing light. If we are on the path that He has called us to, the light in our life will grow brighter every day! We must never settle for less than this, and never allow the enemy to rob us of this basic gift from God to His children: Light!

SYMPTOMS OF CONFUSION

One of the first effects of confusion is that it causes us to live in an increasing state of hesitancy. If it is not recognized and overcome, it will grow into a stronghold of fear, depression, and hopelessness. These are not mental states that any Christian should ever be in, so if we are subject to them to any degree, we have a battle to fight, and we can easily win it.

A main goal of confusion is to darken all of our thoughts and perceptions so that we will not walk in faith. It usually starts in an area of our life that is very important for what God is doing with us. For example, we may have great clarity about our job or profession, but be in confusion about how to raise our children or how to have a good relationship to our spouse or church. We then tend to gravitate toward the area of our life where we feel more in control and will start to drift from the area where we have confusion. This causes us to become increasingly devoted to our job, and increasingly separated from family or church. In this way, confusion is often the beginning of the separations and divisions that destroy relationships. This is almost always a primary strategy of the spirit of confusion—to destroy relationships.

It is obvious that if the enemy is specifically targeting a relationship, it is usually because of the importance of that relationship. Therefore, we must determine that the area, or relationship, that is being attacked by confusion is probably very important to our purpose, so we must not let confusion steal it from us. Sometimes relationships in our life need to change, but "God is not a God of confusion" (1 Cor. 14:33), so if it is His will for a relationship to change He will not use confusion to do it. We therefore must learn to fight for everything and every relationship that is being attacked by confusion.

The key to keeping confusion out of our relationships is to walk uprightly in them. In Proverbs 4:18, it is "the path of the righteous" that gets brighter and brighter. When we allow unrighteousness to enter a relationship, we have opened the door wide for confusion, and it will usually bring many evil friends. Therefore, having a clear definition of righteousness is basic to the clarity that overcomes confusion. Compromising biblical standards of morality and integrity will open us to confusion, and our relationships to destruction.

We must also keep in mind that almost all human relationships will be difficult at times. Even when there were just two brothers on the entire earth they could not get along. However, we can have difficulties without having confusion. Dispatching with the confusion is usually the first step to overcoming the other problems that may exist in our relationships.

DAYLIGHT

In John 8:32, Jesus said, "You will know the truth, and the truth will make you free." The normal Christian life is one of increasing light and clarity because the normal Christian life is one of growing in truth. The purpose of this study is to illuminate the truth about the causes of confusion and to unravel any jumbled thinking and replace it with truth so that we can clearly see the course that is set before us. A basic goal of our life should be clarity of thought because that means that the truth is becoming more clear to us. This will enable us to walk with increasing confidence and boldness, as well as success, in all that we do.

The Main Door of Confusion

Though our problems in this world can become very complicated, the way out of them is usually very simple. However, "simple" and "easy" do not necessarily mean the same thing. To be obedient to our calling as Christians is a simple matter, but difficult to do. Even so, it is always ultimately much easier to obey and do what is right than it is not to.

Simple obedience to the Lord and living by His Word is the ultimate way out of confusion. Compromising what we know is right is to depart from "the path of the righteous" and is the biggest open door to confusion in our life. So our goal must be to know the truth, and obey it.

This does not necessarily imply that if we are in confusion we are in disobedience to the Lord or doing something unrighteous. There are other causes of confusion that we will cover later. However, disobedience to the truth that we know is the most common open door of confusion. If this is the open door to it in our life, then it is a simple matter to get rid of it—obey the truth.

If there is unrighteousness in our life we must honestly and openly admit to it and repent of it, which means to turn away from it, if we are going to be free of confusion. As we are told in First John 1:9, "If we confess our sins, He is faithful and righteous to forgive us our sins and to cleanse us from all unrighteousness." As soon as we do this we can expect clarity to come because we have returned to the "path of the righteous" that is one of ever-increasing light.

Of course this does not mean that we will not have problems, but both the nature of any problems and the solution for overcoming them will become increasingly clear to us if we stay on the path. Clarity of vision is fundamental to every life that is on the path of righteousness. Sin and unrighteousness will always blur our vision and open us to confusion. This is why Proverbs 4:19 states, "The way of the wicked is like darkness; they do not know over what they stumble."

If unrighteousness has gotten into your life, it has probably not only blurred your vision, but made inroads for confusion into other areas of your life as well. That is why First John 1:9 says that if we confess our sins He will "cleanse us from all unrighteousness," which will also bring us clarity in every area where we have had confusion.

THE STRATEGY

Understanding our enemy, confusion, is the first step to defeating it and is actually the biggest part of the battle. However, after that we must have resolve and perseverance to fight it on every front until it is completely defeated and driven from our life. In Second Kings 13 there is an interesting story that illustrates what we must now resolve to do.

In this story a king of Israel came to the prophet Elisha to inquire as to whether he should give battle to a certain enemy. Elisha told him to take his bow and arrows and strike the ground. The king did this three times. The prophet became angry with him saying that he should have struck the ground five or six times, but because he had only struck it three times he would only defeat his enemy three times. Such prophetic antics may be hard to understand, but the point is that when we fight against an enemy we need to strike it as many times as it takes to completely defeat it. If we only partially defeat it we will likely have to continue fighting it for the rest of our life—it will keep coming back to us.

It is for this reason that there are some principles that we will strike repeatedly in this study. It has been proven that most people need considerable repetition for retention of a thought or idea. It then takes even more repetition to actually change behavior. For this reason, recent management studies now recommend that important directives be issued at least four times in writing and verbally to ensure compliance. With each repetition the probability of retention is greatly increased. We not only want retention of the truth, but we want to continue repeating it as often as it takes to change our behavior.

If the repetitions included in this study are not enough, reread the booklet until your victory is complete. You may also want to reread it periodically just to be sure that certain things have not crept back in. Whenever we cast the enemy out of our life he does try to return (see Matt. 12:43-45). Our goal is first to get free, and then stay free!

As you may have already concluded, our keynote verse for being delivered from confusion is Proverbs 4:18. It is one of our "arrows" that we are going to keep striking the ground with until we have the total victory. Other arrows are verses that follow this one in Proverbs 4, so let's take the time to read over them carefully here:

> But the path of the righteous is like the light of dawn, that shines brighter and brighter until the full day. The way of the wicked is like darkness; they do not know over what they stumble. My son, give attention to my words; incline your ear to my sayings. Do not let them depart from your sight; keep them in the midst of your heart. For they are life to those who find them, and health to all their body. Watch over your heart with all diligence, for from it

flow the springs of life. Put away from you a deceit-ful mouth, and put devious speech far from you. Let your eyes look directly ahead and let your gaze be fixed straight in front of you. Watch the path of your feet and all your ways will be established. Do not turn to the right nor to the left; turn your foot from evil (Prov. 4:18-27).

If you are in a battle with confusion, I recommend that you read this text every day for awhile, endeavoring to walk in the truth herein stated. Keep beating the ground with these arrows until you have completely defeated your enemy —confusion.

Building a Fortress of Truth

Crucial to walking in the light so that your life is devoid of confusion is walking in a sound, biblical truth. One of the biblical texts that explains how this is done is Matthew 16:13-18:

> Now when Jesus came into the district of Caesarea Philippi, He was asking His disciples, "Who do people say that the Son of Man is?" And they said, "Some say John the Baptist; and others, Elijah; but still others, Jeremiah, or one of the prophets." He said to them, "But who do you say that I am?" Simon Peter answered, "You are the Christ, the Son of the living God." And Jesus said to him, "Blessed are you, Simon Barjona, because flesh and blood did not reveal this to you, but My Father who is in heaven. I also say to you that you are Peter, and upon this rock I will build My church; and the gates of Hades will not overpower it.

Some have interpreted this to mean that Peter is the rock that the Lord is building His Church on, but a closer examination of this text reveals otherwise. The Greek word that is translated "Peter" is *petros*, which means a piece of rock or a stone. The Greek word that is translated "rock" in this text is *petra*, which is actually a feminine version that literally means "a mass of rock." The rock that the Church is being built upon that the gates of hell cannot prevail against is the revelation from the Father of who Jesus is.

No one can come to the Son unless the Father draws him (see John 6:44). It is the revelation from above that is the rock that all true faith must be built on if it is to stand against the storms that will surely come against it. Ideals and intellectual conclusions can be stolen from us, but when the Father Himself reveals a matter it is a rock in our life that cannot be easily moved. So it is not persuasive arguments from men that lead to true faith—it must be a revelation from the Father of who Jesus is. We are dependent on the Holy Spirit, whom the Father has sent to testify of the Son, for all true illumination.

This is why First John 2:27 says, "His anointing teaches you about all things." Even though I obviously believe that the principles in this study are true, I know that they will accomplish nothing unless the reading of them is accompanied by the Holy Spirit who anoints your study. He was sent to lead us into "all truth," and His anointing is absolutely required for the impartation of spiritual truth.

The fall and all of our human problems are basically the result of man trying to live without God, and the very nature of our redemption should teach us that we need God for everything, especially understanding. For this reason it is not enough for you to just read and try to understand the principles of this book. You must do it in fellowship with the Lord, praying and seeking His help every step of the way. The ultimate deliverance from confusion is to live in His light.

For this reason the Lord is likewise saying to each of us "Blessed are you _____ [insert your name here] because flesh and blood did not reveal this to you, but My Father who is in heaven...and upon this rock [revelation that comes from the Father] I will build My church; and the gates of hell shall not overpower it." If we have perceived who Jesus is it is a blessing, a gift, and not our own achievement. When we receive a revelation from the Father, it is a rock that no amount of human pressure or persuasion can steal from us. That does not mean that all of hell will not try, but faith built on this rock will stand and prevail.

The fortress that we have as a bastion against confusion, or any other assault from hell, is a revelation of who Jesus is. He is above all rule, authority, and dominion. He has prevailed over sin and the devil, and to the degree that we abide in Him and keep our faith in Him, we too will prevail.

Some have wrongly tried to build their lives on a faith in their faith instead of faith in who Jesus is. Our faith is not to be in our faith, but in the person of Jesus Christ—who He is and what He has already accomplished for us. Walking in the light is to walk with *the* Light, Jesus.

Knowing Your Shepherd

In John 10:4 the Lord said concerning Himself as the Good Shepherd, "When he puts forth all his own, he goes ahead of them, and the sheep follow him because they know his voice." It is clear in this verse that if we are His sheep we will know His voice. We follow Him because we know His voice. It could be said that we follow Him to the degree that we know His voice. One of the devil's most effective ploys has been to make the very concept of how to know the will of the Lord a confusing issue to many Christians. Therefore we must address this if we are to be free from confusion.

Even though the matter of knowing the Lord's voice has been made confusing to many, it is a relatively simple matter. Most of the confusion around this is the result of the enemy being able to complicate it. How simple is it? How many people can you recognize by looking at their hand? Their foot? Or any other part of the body? There are basically two things by which we recognize others—their face and their voice. The same is true with the Lord. We must therefore seek His face and to know His voice.

I could pick my wife's voice out of any crowd. I can do this because we have been together so much that I know her voice and can easily distinguish it from any other. The same is the key to knowing the Lord's voice—simply spending time with Him. The increasing light that is the path of the righteous is an increasing revelation of the Son of God. As we behold His glory more and more we too are changed into His same image, as we are told in Second Corinthians 3:18:

> But we all, with unveiled face, beholding as in a mir-
> ror the glory of the Lord, are being transformed into
> the same image from glory to glory, just as from the
> Lord, the Spirit.

It is not enough to just see His glory if we are going to be changed into His same image—we must see His glory with "an unveiled face." Confusion is what places many of the veils upon our faces so that His glory is distorted when we behold it, and therefore we are changed into a distorted image of Him. This is the primary reason why so many Christians are so un-Christlike. As we proceed, we will try to define and then strip away the veils that are clouding the vision of so many.

THE COMPLICATION OF THE DEVIL VERSUS THE SIMPLICITY OF DEVOTION TO CHRIST

Besides overcomplicating how we recognize the Lord's voice, it is a primary strategy of the devil to overly complicate everything that he can. This is a primary way that he spreads confusion. Complication and confusion are coworkers in the devil's strategy. Therefore, we must heed the warning of Second Corinthians 11:3:

But I am afraid that, as the serpent deceived Eve by his craftiness, your minds will be led astray from the simplicity and purity of devotion to Christ.

The words "led astray" in this verse are sometimes translated "beguiled" or "bewitched." It is no accident that witchcraft is a complicated hodgepodge of patterns, formulas, and incantations. This is the way that the devil likes to be sought, and he will usually only give his power to those who are willing to jump through all of the hoops. It is exactly contrary to the simplicity of how God is approached—simple faith in the Son of God will issue you right into His presence.

As this verse above implies, pure devotion to the Lord is a primary antidote to the way that the enemy seeks to lead our minds astray, for which his primary weapon is confusion. To the degree that we keep our devotion to Him simple and pure, confusion will find no place in our life.

We should also note here that Eve was led astray by the serpent's "craftiness." Craftiness could be defined as a tendency to bend the rules and get away with it. If that kind of mentality is in our life, it will likely become a stronghold for confusion to enter. This tendency will greatly complicate our life with many confusing problems. If our goal is anything but pure obedience, pure devotion to Christ, we will be open to confusion. We should therefore not want to bend the rules, nor seek to push them to their limits, but rather to know them so that we can obey them.

The devil caused the first fall by getting Eve to question God. He asked her a simple question, "Did God really say that?" The first step toward a fall, and confusion, is simply to begin questioning the clear directives of God. This was the devil's strategy to complicate something that God had made very simple—"Don't do it."

After the serpent saw that Eve was open to questioning something that God had made clear, it was not hard for him to push her further. He could then get her to begin questioning God's motives. Then it was easy for him to goad her into looking at what she was missing. When she looked at the fruit of the forbidden tree she wondered why a good God would deny her something that looked so good. She obviously concluded that He did not really love them, or He did not mean what He said. This line of reasoning led to the first fall, and many, many more since.

The point is that we are opening a door wide to deception when we question the clear commands of the Lord or His intentions. This does not mean that we cannot ask Him questions or wonder why. However, there is a big difference between asking because we want to obey Him and asking questions because we want to disobey. If we are going to stay on the path of righteousness, we must settle in our heart that He is always good, just, righteous, and always has our best interest in mind. He is always wise, and He is always right.

THE NATURE OF LOVE

It is tragic the way that skepticism is now viewed as a foundation for wisdom and necessary for the pursuit of truth. Skepticism is the foundation of a darkened soul, an open door to the devil's heart, and is contrary to faith that is the foundation of a genuine pursuit of truth. In First Corinthians 13:7 we are told that love "believes all things, hopes all things...." This does not mean that love is naive, or that it does not see flaws and mistakes. What it does mean is that love looks for the best in others, and hopes for the best, not the worst. If you are examining another looking for the worst in them, you can be sure that the devil will show it to you, and bend it considerably as he does.

You may think that anyone who lives by the mandate of love in First Corinthians 13 will suffer perpetual disappointment and perpetual hurt. That is very possible. One thing that few realize, and that every Christian needs to settle in their heart and mind, is that being hurt by others is basic to the call of being a Christian. To live in a way that tries to avoid being hurt will divert us from our basic calling and the path of righteousness.

One of the greatest demonstrations of true love is to keep believing in someone after they have disappointed you or hurt you. We are called to take up our cross daily. The cross is the symbol of the greatest injustice that the world has ever witnessed. No one ever deserved the persecution and death that He suffered less than Jesus did. Yet, He came into this world knowing that this was going to happen, and willingly went to the cross for our salvation. He said in John 17:18, concerning those whom He had called, "As You sent Me into the world, I also have sent them into the world." We have actually been sent into the world to experience injustice and yet, like our Savior, to keep on loving and believing in people.

How many of us would earnestly desire to have one more meal with our closest friends if we knew that within hours these people whom we have invested so much in would deny that they even knew us? It is the basic nature of love to love regardless of how those we love return it. This is the way that we are also called to walk. The Lord said in Matthew 10:38-39:

> *And he who does not take his cross and follow after Me is not worthy of Me. He who has found his life will lose it, and he who has lost his life for My sake will find it.*

Now He does not call us to take up our crosses every day to make atonement for others, since His sacrifice alone could do that. However, just as He went to the cross and let people hurt Him even though He was completely innocent, and did it even for the sake of those who were so unjustly killing Him, we must do the same. We are here to demonstrate the cross by suffering injustice for the sake of the very ones who are treating us unjustly. When we do this in the right spirit, rejoicing that we have been counted worthy to suffer for His name's sake just as the apostles did, rather than feeling sorry for ourselves and walking around with a martyr's complex, the power of the Holy Spirit to bring salvation can be released through us.

Possibly the greatest simplifying factor in our lives would be to let love be our motive in all things in place of the self interests that usually motivate us. This would so simplify our life because the Lord promises that if we will seek His interests first, which is His Kingdom, He will take care of everything that concerns us, just as He promises in Matthew 6:31-34:

> Do not worry then, saying, "What will we eat?" or "What will we drink?" or "What will we wear for clothing?" For the Gentiles eagerly seek all these things; for your heavenly Father knows that you need all these things. But seek first His kingdom and His righteousness, and all these things will be added to you. So do not worry about tomorrow; for tomorrow will care for itself. Each day has enough trouble of its own.

One of the greatest sources of anxiety and confusion is our over-concern about the future of our own self-interests. The Lord promises that if we will put the seeking of His Kingdom first, He will take care of all of that for us. This alone can be one of the biggest deconfusing factors in our lives.

Even though we are here to be hurt and suffer injustice at times, there is a way to do this and actually not be hurt. In fact, that is the way that it is supposed to be. How can we be treated unjustly or be hurt by others and not feel it? We are called to be dead to this world. How can a dead man feel hurt or injustice? For us to take up our crosses daily means that we die daily. We accept that all things that happen to us happen for our good just as we are promised in the Scriptures, so we rejoice in all of our trials.

You may say that is certainly easier said than done, but I would say that it is easier done than not doing it. The more dead we are, the easier our life will be! Sounds crazy, but it is sober, profound truth. If our life is not easy, it is because we have not died to the world yet. In this way we are still seeking to save our lives, when it is those who lose their lives for His sake who find true life. One issue that we need to settle is that the Lord is not just trying to change us—He is trying to kill us!

To encourage you a little more, the two most powerful beings in the universe are both trying to kill you! God and the devil both want you dead! However, they have different ways of doing it, and for different reasons. God is trying to set you free and give you more life than you can even imagine, while the devil is trying to shackle you in every way he can so he can steal your life. If you let God do it, you will be resurrected to a life of more glory and power than you can even imagine—and you begin to partake of that resurrection power in this life!

There is also no greater freedom that we can ever know than to be dead to this world. What can you do to a dead man? It is impossible for a dead man to be offended, feel rejected or sorry for himself, or even get angry. It is impossible for a dead man to be confused. If these things are still happening to us, it is only evidence to the degree that we have refused to walk in our most basic calling as Christians—to take up our crosses (die to ourselves) and follow Him.

It is amazing how clear everything becomes when we are dead! If we are dead, all of the confusion caused by our selfish ambitions, pride, and secret desire to sin, vanishes. The greatest open door for the clarity of the Spirit of God is the cross.

«❧10❧»

The Fear of Man
and Confusion

In this chapter we are going to study another main gateway of confusion into our life—living by the fear of man instead of by the fear of the Lord. The "fear of man" is referring to an inordinate fear of man, which is different from the proper respect that we should have for others. The proper respect to others is what we are exhorted to give in Romans 13:7, "Render to all what is due them: tax to whom tax is due; custom to whom custom; fear to whom fear; honor to whom honor."

Believe it or not, the Greek word that is translated "fear" in this text actually means fear! It could have been translated "alarm" or "fright." There is a respect for authority, for the elderly, etc., that we should have. So when I am here speaking of "the fear of man" I am speaking of an inordinate fear of man.

As we addressed in the last chapter, a great deal of the confusion in people's lives can be broken quickly by the resolve to live in the simplicity of pleasing God rather than other people. When we live by the fear of man instead of by the fear of the Lord, we put ourselves into the cauldron of confusion that is constantly stirred by the whims of others or by the fears empowered by our own constantly changing perceptions of what we think others think of us.

In general, people are not consistent enough, or stable enough, for us to put this kind of trust in them. In fact, the whole fallen world is in the grip of the very confusion that we resolved to get free from. Therefore we must begin by freeing ourselves from the world's controls and expectations in every way that it wrongly influences our life and perceptions.

The Lord has made it very clear what He thinks of us and what He expects of us. We can add to this the assurance that He never changes. Therefore to live in the fear of the Lord rather than by the fear of man will dispel most of the confusion that afflicts almost every person.

THE CONFUSION OF HUMAN RELATIONS

No parents are perfect, and even the best ones can, at times, do things that confuse their children. There are times when the children may do something that irritates their parents so that they get a strong reaction from them. The very next day they may do the same thing, but because their parents are in a different mood they may not get a reaction at all. This kind of thing can produce confusion in their life—like trying to play a game when someone is constantly changing the rules on you and not telling you about it.

If confusion or inconsistency is in you, it will come out in your relationship to your children, your spouse, your coworkers, and everyone else. However, we are all this way until we have been perfected in Christ, and I have yet to meet anyone who has fully attained that. Therefore, we must all learn to live in the love that will "cover a multitude of sins," forgiving their inconsistencies just as they are having to forgive ours.

Christians are all in the process of being delivered from the confusion of this world. We therefore should not allow someone's bad day, or a bad action, to ruin our relationship with them. We should also always be thankful that our Father in heaven is not like us. He never changes, and He is working with us to help us to be like Him—which should be our primary goal in life.

There are other causes of confusion that we will address, but the fear of man is certainly one of the most common. It may seem too simplistic now, but the answer to every question we will address in this study will ultimately be to return to the simplicity of devotion to the Lord. Understanding how we allow other people, or influences, to eclipse our devotion to Him and doing His will, and then understanding how we return to the Lord by repentance, is the path to deliverance from confusion, and even more importantly, sin. If we could live our lives only being concerned with what the Lord thinks of us, and not what other people think of us, confusion would have very little access to our life.

However, we must relate to other people even before we are completely delivered from our fears and the confusion they cause. We need to understand that these relationships are a primary tool that the Lord is using to deliver us. He wants us to love others, but the more you love them the more they can have influence over you. However, we are called to love each other much more, while allowing them to control us less. How can we do this?

Basically, we have to do it by not letting other people's expectations control us. As we are told in Second Corinthians 5:14, "For the love of Christ controls us." How different would our lives be if we were controlled by the love of Christ? Not only would our lives become far more simple than they are now, but they would also be much more successful because "love never fails" (1 Cor. 13:8).

However, we must realize that this perfect love of Christ actually casts out all fear, even the fear of man, so that we are not controlled by the expectations or desires of those whom we love. It is because of not understanding this one thing that many people who enter into ministry are so quickly burned out—they start taking the people's yokes instead of the Lord's yoke. Love is not the permission to control. Perfect love cannot be controlled by anyone but God who alone is perfect.

THE DITCH ON THE OTHER SIDE

There is a ditch on either side of the path of life. Many who have fallen into a ditch oversteer when trying to return to the path and end up in the opposite ditch. Repentance does often mean a radical change of direction, but let us be careful not to overcorrect. Let us return to the statements made in the paragraph above and try to respond to them without making an over-correction.

Does what was said in the paragraph above mean that we do not have to respond to human needs? Does this mean that we do not respond even to the needs of those whom we love and who love us? Yes. In fact, it does. First, it is not true love if it is controlling or demanding. Second, we cannot really help anyone and may even contribute to their sin, confusion, or self-pity with our human compassion. If we really want to help someone, we must do it by God's Spirit. This does not mean that God cannot use us to respond to the needs of others, but we must be led by Him to do it or we will be consumed trying to respond to the needs of others in our own strength.

Jesus never responded to human needs—He only did what He saw the Father doing. If He sent us out just as He was sent, it also means that we are supposed to live this same way. We are not called to feed the hungry, but to feed the hungry that He wants us to feed. He does not send us out to heal all of the sick—Even He did not do that. He wants us to heal the sick that He wants us to heal.

Now you may be thinking that this will give many people the license to not respond to other people's needs at all. It is likely that many will take it to that extreme. As Peter said of Paul's teachings, the unstable and untaught distort them. This will always be the case. However, my point about not responding to human needs is not to turn our backs on those in need, as James warned us against, but rather to seek to follow the Lord in our ministry to others—not the wants, or expectations, of others.

When Jesus told His disciples who were looking at 5,000 hungry people, "You give them something to eat," He empowered them to do it, multiplying their resources. When He directs us to meet anyone's needs, He will empower us to do it, and when He does this we can count on our resources going a lot further than if we try to do it on our own.

Of course, many are asking how do we know the ones that the Lord is leading us to help. Simple—we have to know His voice. Remember, His sheep "follow Him because they know His voice" (John 10:4). Getting to know His voice is not complicated. It is based on simply spending time with Him.

Let us also understand that when we determine not to be controlled by other people's expectations, but rather by the love of Christ, this does not mean that we rebel against our boss because we are not going to let their expectations of us control us. We must endeavor to live by Colossians 3:23-24, "Whatever you do, do your work heartily, as for the Lord rather than for men, knowing that from the Lord you will receive the reward of the inheritance. It is the Lord Christ whom you serve." If we have made the commitment to take a job, we will therefore seek in every way to do the best possible job because of our love for the Lord—whom we are ultimately working for—and because of the love that He has given to us for the people we work for and with.

If we love others, we will also be understanding of why they may not react to us with consistency. We will have an understanding of the confusion in this world that they are having to constantly battle. We will therefore endeavor to be consistent in our relationship to them whether they are or not. This we do because of our love for them, and love loves whether it is rewarded or not. Therefore our goal in all of our relationships should be the simplicity of love that does not waver, even when it is at times rejected or hurt.

As we begin to walk in the consistency that comes from following the One in whom there is no inconsistency or shadow of turning, we will become a rock of refuge in the midst of the storms of confusion in this world. Others will trust us more and more, and this trust can become a bridge by which we can help them to find deliverance through Christ. We must also consider that the more confusion and inconsistency that we are faced with in a relationship, the greater the opportunity that we have to demonstrate the love of God that does not waver.

GOOD FEAR AND BAD FEAR

If we are living by the pure and holy fear of the Lord, we will not fear anything else on this earth. If we live by the fear of the Lord, we will not be controlled by the fear of man or any other fear. When we are not controlled by the fear of man, we can give all men the honor and respect that is due to them, which is a biblical command, but we will do it with the grace and dignity that is befitting sons and daughters of the King of kings.

I have learned to be wary of those who give too much honor to men, and those who do not give honor to whom honor is due, as we are commanded in Romans 13:7. Those who refuse to do the latter often claim that they are not going to worship men or live by the fear of man. I obviously agree that we should not do this, but that does not mean that we do not give the respect and honor that is due to others. In fact, one of the primary ways that we honor the Lord is by honoring His authority that He has delegated to others.

Those who go to the extreme of refusing to give any honor to those who deserve it are either immature in their faith, lacking in understanding, or they are some of the most dangerous people of all because of the pride that is controlling them. You will find that these are the kinds of people who actually demand the most respect and honor from others, and will also be the most prone to control and dominate in their relationships with others.

I am not a very formal person. I really don't like to be called "pastor," much less "apostle," "prophet," or "bishop." I ask all of those in our congregations to call me "Rick," and even my own children do at times. However, I appreciate someone calling me by whatever title they think is appropriate until I tell them otherwise. As a leader with a certain amount of influence, I have learned to be wary of those who show me too much respect, and those who do not show me enough—both are usually going to be a problem. It is not that I need this respect or acknowledgment, as I said. I don't even tend to like it, but it reveals to me very accurately where a person is spiritually.

When I was in the military, we were told not to fraternize with those of lesser rank because they would not respect our authority. That may have been true in the military, and it is true in what the Lord called the authority of the Gentiles, but it is not true in the Kingdom. Jesus not only got close to His disciples, but He lived with them. They were right by His side day and night. In the Kingdom, if someone loses respect for us because they get too close to us, then something is wrong with us. If we are who we claim to be, people should respect us more the closer they get to us.

I want my children and my employees to be completely comfortable and free around me, but I also want them to do what I say the first time I say it. We can, and should, have both. I may lean toward being too casual, but I am far more alarmed when I see a leader's staff or family having an inordinate fear of them, which is usually demonstrated by a humiliating groveling in their presence. I have learned that those who tend to be the most demanding of having others recognize their title or position are usually the least deserving of that title or position.

One of the most devastating sources of confusion is found in Isaiah 9:16, "For those who guide this people are leading them astray; and those who are guided by them are brought to confusion." One does not have to look back far into the history of the church to see that the majority of the confusion that has come into the Body of Christ has come from leaders who do not walk in righteousness. We will elaborate on this a little more in the next chapter, but for now we must demand the highest standards of morality and integrity from those whom we recognize as leaders in the Church or we will continue to be subject to the terrible confusion that has rested upon the Church since the first century. The over-concern with titles and positions is a symptom of something basically awry in a person's life and should be a disqualification from leadership.

It is interesting how the King of kings did not demand anyone to call Him by a title. The ones who have the most real authority will inevitably be the least demanding of others to recognize it. Those who have true spiritual authority have received it from above, and it is from above that they get their encouragement. Those who know that they were sent from above will not be overly encouraged or discouraged by what other people think of them. Those who are inordinately in pursuit of encouragement from the recognition of other men should not be in spiritual leadership. At the same time we must learn to show the proper respect for all of the Lord's servants, ambassadors, and the leaders that He has chosen. We must learn to show the proper respect for others without worshiping or having an inordinate fear of them.

A major open door to confusion will come from trying to serve two masters. This confusion is multiplied when we try to please everyone. Remember, anything with more than one head is a monster. In First Corinthians 11:3 we are told, "But I want you to understand that Christ is the head of every man." Others can be our leaders, have authority and influence with us, but only One can be our Head.

One of the primary ways that confusion enters our life is when the Lord speaks to us, or leads us in a certain way, and we begin to be concerned about what other people think. Because of this we give honor to others first because of the biblical command to do so, out of respect for the Lord and all authority that He has delegated on the earth.

WHOSE AMBASSADOR ARE YOU?

In Second Corinthians 5:20, Paul wrote, "Therefore, we are ambassadors for Christ...." In biblical times to be an ambassador of a nation was the highest honor one could receive from the king or emperor. There were no phones, fax machines, or email, so oftentimes kings could not communicate with their ambassadors for months at a time. Therefore, only those who were the very best friends of the king, those he knew were of one mind with him and would only represent his interests, would be chosen as ambassadors. Even then ambassadors were recalled every two years because it was felt that after that period of time they would begin to be more sympathetic to the country they were sent to than the one they had been sent from.

Because the Lord does not recall His ambassadors every two years, we must check our hearts continually to be sure that we are representing His interests rather than man's. That is why Paul wrote in Galatians 1:10, "If I were still trying to please men, I would not be a bond-servant of Christ." Think about it. To the degree that we are seeking to please men instead of Christ we will fail to be His bondservant.

In Luke 16:15, the Lord said to the Pharisees, "You are those who justify yourselves in the sight of men, but God knows your hearts; for that which is highly esteemed among men is detestable in the sight of God." Consider that. What is highly esteemed among men is detestable in God's sight! I think that the reverse is also usually true—that which is highly esteemed with God is detestable in the sight of men. We have a major choice to make in our life. Someone is going to detest what we do, God or men. Who do we want it to be? As the Lord said in Luke 6:26, "Woe to you when all men speak well of you, for their fathers used to treat the false prophets in the same way."

SPIRITUAL ADULTERY

If on your wedding day your spouse-to-be came up to you and said, "Darling, I love you so much that I am going to be faithful to you 364 days a year! I only want one day a year to mess around," would you continue with the wedding? With that in mind consider James 4:4:

> You adulteresses, do you not know that friendship with the world is hostility toward God? Therefore whoever wishes to be a friend of the world makes himself an enemy of God.

We have been betrothed to Christ. We cannot be married to Him and married to the world too. It is not a matter of us being mostly His and that we very seldom mess around with the world. His bride is going to be a pure, chaste virgin, so we cannot determine to be married to the world until He returns and then switch. We have a choice to make—who are we going to be married to, the world or Christ? It cannot be both. To try to serve both is not only a wide open door to confusion, it is a wide open door to eternal grief.

THE DESTROYER OF FAITH

In John 5:44, Jesus asked what should be considered one of the ultimate questions, "How can you believe, when you receive glory from one another and you do not seek the glory that is from the one and only true God?" The Greek word that is translated "glory" here could have been translated "respect" or "honor." Previously we discussed how we should give respect to those to whom it is due, but here we are profoundly challenged not to seek it from men. As the question implies, to do so is probably the number one destroyer of true faith.

SUMMARY

In First Kings 17:1, we have the dramatic entrance of one of the greatest prophets who ever lived, Elijah. In what appears to have been his first prophetic statement, he declares what was probably a main reason why he was trusted with so much authority when he said, "As the Lord, the God of Israel lives, before whom I stand...." Even though Elijah was standing before the king at the time, it was the Lord he was really standing before. It was the Lord, not men, not even the king, whom Elijah lived his life before. To the degree that we can do this we will be delivered from confusion and can be trusted with real authority.

Again, normal Christianity is a life of ever-increasing light, peace, and joy. We must resolve that we will not continue to settle for anything less than the joy and peace that is the inheritance of every citizen of the Kingdom of God.

It is not normal for a Christian to be in confusion. Christ is the "Light of the World." How can we be in confusion if we are abiding in Him? We must recognize confusion as evidence that we have either been distracted from our place in Him, or we are under an assault of the enemy who intends to do just that—so our options are to repent or fight. The purpose of the rest of this study is to help us determine which it should be, and how to do either one when it is needed.

((◎11◎))

Pride and Sin

Man was created as the most majestic of God's creatures on the earth. We stand and walk upright. We were created to rule over the earth and all of its other creatures. We were also created in the image of God. Every human being is marvelous, even to the angels that we were created a little lower than. We were created to have a special fellowship with God Himself. God has even chosen to make His dwelling place with man. For these reasons it is easy for man to become proud. However, because of the fall we will also forever have a reason to be humble. God did not cause man to fall—that was our own choice—but it will serve to allow man to be exalted to the high place of being the abode of God because we will forever have reason to fully understand our need and dependence on His grace and redemption.

Pride is one of the biggest open doors to confusion. As we are told in Proverbs 11:2, "When pride comes, then comes dishonor, but with the humble is wisdom." The Hebrew word that is translated "dishonor" here is *qalown* (kaw-lone'), which is also translated "disgrace," "dishonor," "ignominy," "reproach," "shame," and "confusion." These are all of the consequences of the fall. If we are to walk in the honor and dignity of our calling, we must begin with having the humility to know how desperately we are dependent on the grace and redemption of God that is available to us at the cross. To walk in the light and to be able to see where we are going will require humility. We must start to recognize this deadly enemy—pride—and repent of it.

We must also begin to demand humility from those whom we will recognize as leaders in the Church or we will continue to experience the "disgrace, dishonor, ignominy, reproach, shame, and confusion" that has been the domain of the Church for so long now. Leaders lead people to where they themselves are. They impart to those who are under them what is in them. If they are walking in pride, their church members will end up in pride and the confusion that it causes.

If we are going to be free from confusion we must be consistent in our own hearts, which is to walk in reality and truth. To begin to live by this reality and truth, it is is important to recognize that you probably have a problem with confusion or you would not be reading this book. This is important to admit because this acknowledgment can be a big part of the battle to overcome confusion. (Obviously I had a problem with it or I would not have had to learn these truths that I am sharing here.) This is also important to admit because doing so will begin to break the power of one of the most powerful entry ways of confusion—pride. Therefore James 4:6b-8 is a crucial truth in this battle against confusion, as well as in our overall pursuit of God:

> *Therefore it says, "God is opposed to the proud, but gives grace to the humble." Submit therefore to God. Resist the devil and he will flee from you. Draw near to God and He will draw near to you. Cleanse your hands, you sinners; and purify your hearts, you double-minded.*

The main reason that we usually refuse to acknowledge a problem is pride, and this is the pride that will even cause God to resist us. As Peter Lord likes to say, "The main thing is to keep the main thing the main thing," and the main thing we need in our life is God's grace. Since He gives grace to the humble, pursuing humility is one of the most worthwhile devotions we can have.

Many of the complications in most people's lives are the direct result of pride. For this reason, in many cases confusion will start to be dispelled the moment we determine to humble ourselves in a matter. When we catch this truth, as well as the even more important one that God gives His grace to the humble, we will begin to spend much more time seeking to humble ourselves than we do trying to exalt ourselves like we usually do. This alone can send great clouds of darkness fleeing. Those who start to know the true value of the grace and favor of God will not care at all what they look like before people—their pursuit will be the grace of God that comes with humility. In fact, as this truth becomes a reality to us, we will start devoting much more time to looking smaller, trying to humble ourselves every opportunity that we get.

As the verses above also reveal, humbling ourselves is how we both submit to God and resist the devil. Pride caused the first fall, the fall of the devil himself, and it has caused most of the falls from grace since. Therefore, whenever we humble ourselves we are submitting to God and resisting the devil at the same time. When we start doing this the devil will flee from us because he knows that we are about to receive the grace and favor of the Lord that is directly convertible into the spiritual currency of spiritual authority.

Just being a Christian in this world requires a certain amount of humility. The pride that most of the people of this world live by compels them to think that belief in God is a crutch. I fully agree that it is because I know that I need a crutch. In fact, at the end of this age things will be in such a mess that all of humanity, and the rest of creation, will know for sure that we cannot run things without God—we need Him! I thank Him daily that He is willing to be our crutch!

The same is true of all men whether they acknowledge it or not. Not one of us could even draw a breath without His grace. The greatest genius may be an atheist, but they would not be a genius without the abilities that God gave to them. Pride in our own mental abilities gives an opening to the most base and ridiculous confusion that has come from man, or upon man.

For example, if you went for a walk on the beach one morning and found a brand new Mercedes, complete with gas in the tank and manuals in the glove compartment, and someone tried to tell you that the ocean made that car and deposited it on the beach, you would consider them an idiot more on the level of an oyster than a human being. Even so, that is exactly the kind of ridiculous theories that naturalists have tried to compel modern men to believe—and most modern men have swallowed it!

Consider this: The extensive, sequential knowledge in the DNA of a single living cell is far more complex than what was required to make the Mercedes. For the ocean to have produced a single living cell would be a greater miracle than if it had created this car, with the gas, keys, manuals, and everything else in it! However, even the most dull among us would have trouble believing that the ocean even created a tire that we found on the beach—how can we go on believing the kind of foolishness that naturalists are proposing? However, naturalists are trying to convince the world that not only did a living cell come from the ocean, but zillions of similar miracle accidents, all in perfect timing, took place to develop life as we know it without a single mishap—and all of this happened by accident!

For these "brilliant scientists" to believe the foolishness that naturalism promotes, we can only attribute it to a confusion of the highest level. How could a person observe day after day the miracles of creation—freely admitting that all of our computers combined are still not powerful enough to even compute the odds that just one of the miracles could happen by itself—and yet still believe that this all just happened by accident unless they are under one of the darkest clouds of confusion? Even the most simple observer in honest natural science will conclude that there was a Superior Intelligence far beyond anything we can yet even begin to measure that brought forth all that we know—therefore there had to be a Creator.

The pride of man in such forms as humanism is the source of some of the darkest forms of confusion on the earth. It was a nationalistic pride that led some of the world's most noble and brilliant people, the Germans, to fall to the tragic delusions of the Nazis. Such pride will open the door to delusions in our churches, our companies, and even our families. Any good that we are or have that does not acknowledge it as being the grace of God will be a wide open door for delusion and deception.

SIN AND CONFUSION

We have already superficially covered this source of confusion, but we need to look at it in a little more depth to close this major source of confusion into our lives. As stated, there is some repetition throughout this study by design. There are also overlaps and interrelationships between the sources of confusion that merit the review of some of these principles.

As stated, the first thing that the serpent did to cause Adam and Eve to sin is to get them to question the clear commandment of God. Then it tried to get them to question God's intentions. This is still one of the devil's most effective strategies in causing God's people to stumble—blur the commandment, and then get us to rationalize God's intention for giving it. Just giving into this line of thinking can open the door wide for confusion into our life.

The devil dwells in darkness. That is his domain. For him to bring us into bondage under his domain he must first cloud our vision, and then darken it. Getting us to compromise the clear mandates of God is the primary way that he does this, and it will always lead to our bondage to the devil and his ways.

Martin Luther once made an interesting statement. He said, "If you sin, sin boldly!" He was not encouraging people to willfully sin. He was encouraging them to call sin "sin," and not to try to rationalize it. If you rationalize it you will never repent of it.

When we sin we usually go through the same process that Adam and Eve did after their sin. First we try to hide. Then we try to blameshift. Adam declared that it was the woman's fault, and the woman tried to blame the serpent. This only adds to our confusion. The only way out of the confusion that is the result of sin is to repent of the sin. To repent you have to acknowledge that you did something wrong. God does not forgive excuses—He forgives sin. He will forgive our sin if we will acknowledge it and repent of it. To be free we must stop trying to hide our sin, and stop trying to justify it—we must repent.

Do not ever allow the devil to get you to start compromising the clear word of the Lord. You will always be much better off if you don't do what you know is wrong, but if you sin, as Martin Luther encouraged, be honest about it. For many people this one thing can so dramatically deliver them from the confusion in their life that it is like turning a hurricane into a bright sunny day.

If Adam and Eve had run to God instead of trying to hide from Him and shift blame, the whole world would probably be a far less dark and violent place than it is today. They would still have died, and we would still have needed the atonement of the cross, but it would not have been as bad. My point is that there are always bad consequences for sin, and we cannot escape them, but we can lessen them. We will always be much better off if we run to God when we sin instead of away from Him. He will forgive us and cover the sin if we repent of it. As we read earlier in First John 1:9-10:

> *If we confess our sins, He is faithful and righteous to forgive us our sins and to cleanse us from all unrighteousness. If we say that we have not sinned, we make Him a liar and His word is not in us.*

One of the ways that the devil is trying to prepare the world for his "deep darkness" is to blur distinctions, because when something is distinct it is clear. Take the distinctions between men and women. The Lord made men and women to be different so that they would need each other, not so that they would be in perpetual conflict. Our differences complement each other, causing us to fit together so that it takes both together to make a whole. However, I will never be able to become one with my wife by making her into man. To become one I must recognize and appreciate the way that the Lord made us different.

One of the main social reasons why there is such a drive to blur the distinctions between men and women, and to refuse other forms of stereotyping, is because this has often been used to wrongly discriminate against a people group. The differences between men and women, or between races, nations, and cultures, should not be a cause of wrongful discrimination, but to refuse to recognize the differences is to be blind to reality. Though justice is often portrayed as being blind, true and ultimate justice will never come from being blind, but rather from acknowledging truth and reacting to it with justice in our heart.

There are similar movements to blur the distinctions between good and evil, and between different religions. These will say such things as "we all worship the same god." That is not true, and though we should show dignity and respect for all people who are made in the image of God, the god served by any other religion is not our same God.

It was by trying to serve other gods along with Jehovah that Israel repeatedly fell into confusion and bondage, and was ultimately driven from their promised land. If we begin to compromise the One we serve for the sake of peace or being accepted by other people, we are in fact denying the One we claim to serve and are opening ourselves to the ultimate deception and confusion. The ultimate sin is to deny our God to worship other gods.

In Amos 3:3 the question is asked, "Can two walk together, unless they are agreed?" (NKJV) This is an important question, but one that is often misunderstood. Many have interpreted it as meaning that we cannot walk with anyone unless we are in perfect agreement with them. If we carry that to its logical conclusion then no human being would ever be able to have any kind of relationship with another human being. What this verse does mean is that we can walk together with others in the things that we do agree on.

For example, I recognize the profound difference between Islam and Christianity. However, I do have more in common with one who at least believes in God than I do with an atheist. I could very easily join with Muslims, or those of other religions, to protect religious liberty. I would "walk together with them" in pursuing or protecting the freedom of worship. However, I would not to any degree compromise the fact that there is only one true God, Jesus is His Son, and no one can come to God except through the atonement made by the Son. I would not worship with anyone who did not believe these basics.

Among Christians, we should be able to walk together in many areas, but not necessarily in everything. If we would walk together in the things that we do agree on, we would probably start to trust each other enough to at least listen to each other's views on things we may not agree on. When we do this we will usually find that our positions and beliefs are not as far from each other as we may have thought, and soon we are more open to hear more from each other. Often we will just find out that though we disagree, it is not as big of a deal as we may have made of it.

However, to avoid opening the door to confusion we should never compromise our convictions for the sake of unity, and we will never have to for true unity. One of the most basic characteristics of true humility is to be teachable. To be teachable is to be open and willing to learn, but that does not mean compromise. We should always be humble enough to change our convictions when we are clearly shown that they are wrong, but never compromise them. To compromise is to surrender a position for the sake of political expediency, which will be the basis of a false unity at best. To compromise the truth that we know is also sin, and it will open the door to confusion. The basic commodity that our life as Christians is built on is truth.

《C12》

Spiritual Attacks
and Confusion

Another main source of confusion in Christians' lives is simply from a spiritual attack. We can allow inroads for an evil spirit of confusion by our disobedience, but Christians can also suffer attacks from a spirit of confusion that is the result of their doing what is right, not what is wrong. However, these can be easily distinguished and resisted. As we are delivered from confusion and walk in the path of the righteous that has ever-increasing light, we will more and more quickly discern the source of confusion and be able to shut that gate of hell that it is using to come through.

First Corinthians 14:33 tells us that "God is not a God of confusion but of peace." In place of confusion we should have the peace of God in our life. It is also the peace of God that begins to dispel the confusion. God never uses confusion against His people, and no confusion that His people suffer ever comes from Him. Therefore confusion is not the normal state for any Christian to be in. This does not mean that Christians don't have trials and get attacked with confusion, but it is never coming from God, so we must resist it until it flees.

Nor does this mean that we cannot go through periods when we are not sure which direction to take, or what decision to make in a matter. However, there is a difference between not being sure about something and being in confusion about it.

If confusion is the result of an attack from the enemy, just discerning it will begin to dispel it. Remember, the enemy dwells in darkness because his main power is the power of deception. So, every time we shine the light on him, or his work, it begins to break his power. Then, as soon as we begin to resist him, he will flee. If confusion is the result of our own mistakes, or sin, we must recognize them and repent of them so that the gate that confusion is using to gain access into our lives can be closed. If it is the result of our allowing the fear of man to control us, we must repent of making men idols that we put our trust and hope in instead of God. If it is the result of a spiritual attack, we must recognize it and resist the devil until he flees.

The spirit of confusion is an enemy of truth and light; it is a thief that has come to steal our life. The spirit of confusion will try to rob us of our very purpose for being here. To be free of confusion we must determine to live within the peace and joy that mark the borders of the Kingdom of God. We must resolve that we will not allow ourselves to be distracted from the domain of our God for a single day to be drawn into the enemy's domain of darkness.

As previously stated, for various reasons everyone will have to deal with confusion from time to time, and it does not necessarily mean that a demonic spirit is attacking us every time we get confused about something. However, Christians are called to abide in Christ, not in confusion. Again, we should consider any confusion as an alarm that something is not right, and it needs to be put right.

A growing source of spiritual confusion in our times is from witchcraft. As we have published much on this subject, including a booklet in this same stronghold series, we will only touch on it briefly here, borrowing from the previous work.

The practice of witchcraft has dramatically increased throughout the world in recent years. One of the expressed goals of this movement is to dilute, subjugate, and destroy biblical Christianity. Many Christians are presently suffering attacks in some form from those who practice witchcraft. Discerning the nature of these attacks and knowing how to overcome them is becoming crucial for all believers.

We are exhorted not to be ignorant of the enemy's schemes (see 2 Cor. 2:11). Peter warned us, saying, "Be of sober spirit, be on the alert. Your adversary, the devil, prowls around like a roaring lion, seeking someone to devour. But resist him, firm in your faith" (1 Pet. 5:8-9a). Understanding satan's schemes significantly increases our advantage in the battle. The entire church age has been one of spiritual warfare that is increasing as we approach the end of the age. Those who refuse to acknowledge the reality of this warfare and fight are being overcome. Every Christian is living behind enemy lines. Presently, the whole world does lie in the power of the evil one. We are here to destroy his works—we are here to fight!

Satan is now being cast out of the heavens and down to the earth where he is coming with great wrath. This is the reason for the increasing confusion upon the earth among nations. Even so, we need not fear—He who is in us is much greater than he who is in the world. He who is least in the Kingdom of God has more power than any antichrist.

But just as the greatest military power today is vulnerable if it does not recognize the enemy's attack, we too are vulnerable if we do not recognize satan's schemes. The only way that he can defeat us is by our own ignorance or complacency. As we maintain our position in Christ, take on the full armor of God, and remain vigilant, we will not only stand, but will prevail against the gates of hell.

WHAT IS WITCHCRAFT?

Because we covered this in some depth in the second book of this series, *Overcoming Evil in the Last Days*, here is just a very brief explanation of this for those who did not read the previous book. If you suspect that this is a source of con-fusion in your life, I highly recommend that you read that book as it has been used to help many people, and this is going to be an increasing problem in our times.

Witchcraft is counterfeit spiritual authority; it is using a spirit other than the Holy Spirit to dominate, manipulate, or control others.

The apostle Paul named witchcraft, or "sorcery," as one of the works of the flesh in Galatians 5:20. It does have its ori-gin in the carnal nature though it usually degenerates quickly into demonic power. When we try to use emotional pressure to manipulate others, it is a basic form of witchcraft. When we use hype or soul power to enlist service, even for the work of God, it is witchcraft. When businessmen scheme to find pressure points while pursuing a deal, this too can be witchcraft. Many of the manipulative tactics promoted as sales techniques in marketing are basic forms of witchcraft. Recognizing them, and refusing to use them, is repentance that begins to enable us to be trusted with true spiritual authority.

The basic defense against counterfeit spiritual authority is to walk in true spiritual authority. Establishing our lives on truth and trusting in the Lord to accomplish what concerns us are essential if we are going to be free of the influence and pressure of witchcraft.

It is written that Jesus is seated upon the throne of David. This is of course a metaphor. King David established a position of true spiritual authority that would ultimately issue in the Kingdom of God. David did for spiritual authority what Abraham did for faith. How did David establish a seat of true authority? Basically he refused to take authority or influ-ence for himself, but completely trusted in God to establish him in the position that He had ordained for him.

Any authority, which is influence, that we gain by our own manipulation or self-promotion will be a stumbling block to us and our ability to receive a true commission and author-ity from God. If we are going to walk in true spiritual author-ity, like David, we will have to trust in the Lord to establish us in it, and in His time. As Peter exhorted, "Therefore hum-ble yourselves under the mighty hand of God, that He may exalt you at the proper time" (1 Pet. 5:6).

Witchcraft is rooted in the profound pride whereby a person begins to think that they should be the one in control, and that they have the wisdom and should have the power to enforce their will on others. This is the end result of the most basic rebellion against God and His leadership. Therefore all true spiritual leaders who are appointed by God will have a healthy humility whereby they know that they cannot accomplish what is right without God. They will abhor the thought of doing things in their own wisdom or strength. Those who are self-appointed, or who have fallen from a right relationship with God, will be evident by their pride and arrogance in leadership.

As we discussed earlier, Proverbs 11:2 says, "When pride comes, then comes dishonor, but with the humble is wisdom." Remember also that the Hebrew word that is translated "dis-honor" could also be translated "disgrace," "dishonor," "ignominy," "reproach," "shame," and "confusion." Are these not all of the things that the Church has consistently and repeat-edly been subject to? Can we not trace all of this back to when leadership in the Church was made into a position of privilege and power over others instead of the place of service by servant leaders that it was intended to be?

We will continue to see the Church be subject to the reproach and the resulting confusion until we do what the Lord commended the Ephesian Church for in Revelation 2:2, to "put to the test those who call themselves apostles, and they are not." We might paraphrase this to say "put to the test those who claim to be sent by God and are not." This also implies that we reject them as our leaders. These "false apostles" will be evidenced by their pride, which will always ultimately lead to dishonor and confusion. Because these are counterfeit spiritual authorities we can expect such to use the counterfeit spiritual authority of manipulation, control, and other schemes to accomplish their purpose. We must reject such as these or we will pay the ultimate price of confusion.

«(C)13(Q)»

Other Sources of Confusion

In this chapter we are going to very briefly look at other sources of confusion that are revealed in Scripture.

UNRIGHTEOUS JUDGMENT

Isaiah 59:4 states, "No one sues righteously and no one pleads honestly. They trust in confusion and speak lies; they conceive mischief, and bring forth iniquity." By this we see that there will be confusion when there is evil intent or attempts to plead our case by anything but straightforward honesty. When we try to manipulate others in this way we open our own lives to the same.

This verse is especially addressing lawsuits. Some Christians believe that they should never sue because of First Corinthians 6:5-8:

> I say this to your shame. Is it so, that there is not among you one wise man who will be able to decide between his brethren, but brother goes to law with brother, and that before unbelievers? Actually, then, it is already a defeat for you, that you have lawsuits with one another. Why not rather be wronged? Why not rather be defrauded? On the contrary, you yourselves wrong and defraud. You do this even to your brethren.

First, it was not the apostle's intention here to condemn all lawsuits. Lawsuits were a basic part of the system of justice that God had established in Israel. He was protesting that they were taking their suits before unbelieving judges because there were no trustworthy judges among the believers.

Paul was also saying to the Corinthians that there was a higher way, which was to forgive and accept the wrong. This is what Jesus did when He went to the cross when He could have demanded justice and called on legions of angels to come to His aid. Even so, Paul obviously understood that there are times when one must sue for justice, even before unbelievers, which is what he himself actually did when he sued for justice by appealing to Caesar. However, in his case against the rulers of Israel who were trying to kill him, there was obviously no possibility of going before believers to resolve the matter.

In First Corinthians 6, Paul illuminates what is certainly one of the greatest causes of shame in the Body of Christ today—the fact that there are no judges in the Church. We are told in Psalm 89:14a, "Righteousness and justice are the foundation of Your throne." We have not even been doing well with the righteousness part, but it is rare to ever even hear justice being addressed in the Church, and justice is one of the two foundational pillars of the Lord's throne. If we are going to live in the Kingdom, under the authority of the King, we must have both righteousness and justice established in the Church.

The New Testament Church government was typed after the model of Israel's biblical government. A foundation for that government was established through Moses and was further developed through Joshua and the judges after they had entered their promised land in preparation for the age of the kings that was to be a biblical model for the Kingdom.

The foundation of the civil authority in Israel was from the beginning established on the recognition of elders. One of the primary duties of the elders was to sit in the gates of the cities and act as judges for the people. This is actually supposed to likewise be one of the primary functions of elders in the Church. Paul was lamenting to the Corinthians that they did not have anyone who was actually functioning in this way. Not having this foundation of "justice" established in the Church is probably a major reason why the Corinthians were also having some serious problems in the area of righteousness as well. God's throne, or His authority, will always be built on both of the pillars of righteousness and justice, together.

Obviously it seems that the Church universal is today in the same condition that the Corinthians were in, having no judges, and therefore experiencing continual shame and confusion. This is a subject worthy of a study in itself, and cannot be fully dealt with here, but it is easy to see that it remains a wide open door for confusion in the Church just as it was in Corinth.

GATHERING WITHOUT A PURPOSE

An example of this is found in Acts 19:32, "So then, some were shouting one thing and some another, for the assembly was in confusion and the majority did not know for what reason they had come together."

I have been in some very wonderful meetings when people came together without an agenda to be open to the Lord to move in a unique way. However, for every one of these that I feel really did experience a move of the Holy Spirit there were dozens that ended up in confusion. I have come to the conclusion that if the mature do not take the authority that has been given to them, the immature, the rebellious, and the confused will seize the opportunity to fill the void.

I do believe that it can be a worthy goal for a prayer meeting, home groups, or even a church, to get to the place of spiritual maturity where they all come completely open to the

Spirit to move in their gatherings. However, the key word here is that this can be a worthy "goal." You do not climb a mountain by jumping right to the top—there is a step-by-step ascent. To try to do this with immature believers is opening the door wide to confusion in our meetings.

There is good control as well as bad. Of course, to the rebellious, stubborn, or self-willed, any restraint will be considered a "control spirit." Even so, without the good control, the chaos and confusion in this world would be unbearable. My younger children require much more control and oversight than my older children. It should be this way in the church as well. As a church matures it should need fewer restraints. However, if there is true life in a church it will have a continual influx of new believers who will need a lot of oversight and control in their lives while they mature. If you just throw the meetings open to being "led by the Spirit" you are likely to be led by a spirit you do not want to be led by—confusion.

Getting the mind of the Lord before a meeting and being able to steer it in the right way is just as much being led by the Spirit as anyone who claims to be led spontaneously. In fact, it was the nature of the Lord to see the end from the beginning so it seems that those who are truly maturing in Him should be able to get His mind for a meeting beforehand. A key is to remain humble and flexible enough to always be aware that we "see in part," and "know in part," so there are likely parts to the meeting that God would like to include that we may not be aware of beforehand, so we are open to these.

For the sake of avoiding much frustration and confusion we should always have a purpose for our gatherings, and though we want to always be sensitive to the Spirit and flexible, generally we should have the leadership and discipline to stick to the purpose.

PROPHESYING OUT OF ORDER

Confusion can be the result of prophets prophesying out of order. In First Corinthians 14:31-33 we read, "For you can all prophesy one by one, so that all may learn and all may be exhorted; and the spirits of prophets are subject to prophets; for God is not a God of confusion but of peace, as in all the churches of the saints."

First we see here that "you can all prophesy." The Lord can use anyone at any time to prophesy. In fact, because we "see in part" and "prophesy in part" we are going to need to have more than one prophesying if we are going to get the complete message.

We also see here that "the spirits of the prophets are subject to the prophets." This means that if anyone prophesying loses control of themselves it is their fault! I have heard people say that the Spirit just took over the mind and tongue to give the message through them, or even took over their bodies to make them do strange things as a part of the message, but this is evidence that another spirit other than the Holy Spirit got involved. The "spirits of the prophets are subject to the prophets" because, as this text declares, "God is not a God of confusion." Confusion that is the result of a message that did not come from the Holy Spirit, but rather another spirit, will be the result if we lose control of our own spirits.

JEALOUSY, SELFISH AMBITION, AND CONFUSION

The following text from James 3:11-18 is one of the most important in the Bible for establishing a basic grid for discernment:

Does a fountain send out from the same opening both fresh and bitter water? Can a fig tree, my brethren, produce olives, or a vine produce figs? Nor can salt water produce fresh. Who among you is wise and understanding? Let him show by his good behavior his deeds in the gentleness of wisdom. But if you have bitter jealousy and selfish ambition in your heart, do not be arrogant and so lie against the truth. This wisdom is not that which comes down from above, but is earthly, natural, demonic. For where jealousy and selfish ambition exist, there is disorder [confusion] and every evil thing. But the wisdom from above is first pure, then peaceable, gentle, reasonable, full of mercy and good fruits, unwavering, without hypocrisy. And the seed whose fruit is righteousness is sown in peace by those who make peace.

So we see here that where there is "jealousy and selfish ambition there is disorder [confusion] and every evil thing." Jealousy and selfish ambition are two of the widest open doors to confusion and every other kind of evil. "Every evil thing" is included here because when confusion comes in you can count on it bringing many of its friends.

So how do we counter this? We counter every evil spirit with the Spirit of Christ. It was His nature to humble Himself, leaving His exalted seat of glory to become a man, to live in the most humble circumstances and even give His life for our salvation and ultimate exaltation to be heirs of God with Him. He will allow us to do even greater works than He did now that He has returned to the Father. If we really have the Spirit of Christ, it will be most profoundly exhibited by our willingness to humble ourselves to help save and promote others. The true nature of those who are walking in the Spirit of Christ is that the ones they serve will go farther than they did. In a sense, their ceiling will become the floor for those whom they raise up.

Contrary to this, we know that Jesus was crucified because of envy. Most of the strife and divisions in the

Church throughout history are the result of the same—jealousy and selfish ambition. That is why "the seed whose fruit is righteousness is sown in peace by those who make peace." There is a peace that abides with those who are not being driven by either jealousy or selfish ambition that imparts peace like seeds wherever they go.

This is further summarized in First John 2:5-11 and 3:10-18:

> *But whoever keeps His word, in him the love of God has truly been perfected. By this we know that we are in Him: the one who says he abides in Him ought himself to walk in the same manner as He walked.... The one who says he is in the Light and yet hates his brother is in the darkness until now. The one who loves his brother abides in the Light and there is no cause for stumbling in him. But the one who hates his brother is in the darkness and walks in the darkness, and does not know where he is going because the darkness has blinded his eyes. ...By this the children of God and the children of the devil are obvious: anyone who does not practice righteousness is not of God, nor the one who does not love his brother. For this is the message which you have heard from the beginning, that we should love one another; not as Cain, who was of the evil one and slew his brother. And for what reason did he slay him? Because his deeds were evil, and his brother's were righteous. Do not be surprised, brethren, if the world hates you. We know that we have passed out of death into life, because we love the brethren. He who does not love abides in death. Everyone who hates his brother is a murderer; and you know that no murderer has eternal life abiding in him. We know love by this, that He laid down His life for us; and we ought to lay down our lives*

for the brethren.... Little children, let us not love with word or with tongue, but in deed and truth.

Our ultimate deliverance from confusion will come when we walk in the perfect love of God. This is to know His love for us, and to be a vessel for Him to use to show His love to others. Love simplifies like nothing else ever will. There is no higher calling, or greater power, than the love of God. That is why "love never fails."

14

Order and the Power of God

As we have been somewhat focused on the power of evil, we now want to study the power of God, and how believers have access to that which will easily overcome any power of the enemy.

THE GOD OF ORDER

Exodus 12:38 says that a great "mixed multitude" left the land of Egypt. One of the first administrative purposes of Moses in the wilderness was to establish the congregation in tribal order so that they camped, worshiped, marched, and entered battle with their own tribe, and in the order that God had established.

I have long believed that the Body of Christ has also been so ordered. There are spiritual tribes that the Church is divided into. These transcend denominations, being larger movements within the faith. This is a positive thing, and as we mature it will actually help to bring about the unity of the Body, not detract from it. We may not understand this now, but we will. Just as my human body would be grotesque and deformed if I had all legs and no arms, the beauty and symmetry of the human body is demonstrated by how all of the different parts work together. The Body of Christ will be the same.

We should also note that it was in Egypt, in bondage, that the children of Israel were in disorder. Disorder is a characteristic of satan's domain as we see in Job 10:22, which calls it, "The land of utter gloom as darkness itself, of deep shadow without order, and which shines as the darkness." We also see this stated in James 3:15-16, "This wisdom is not that which comes down from above, but is earthly, natural, demonic. For where jealousy and selfish ambition exist, *there is disorder* and every evil thing."

Two of the most basic contrasts between the Kingdom of God and the domain of darkness is that darkness always results in confusion and disorder, but the Kingdom of God is always moving toward order and harmony. When we came to the Lord it is likely that our lives were in chaos, and it was the work of the Spirit to start bringing order, harmony, and peace into our lives. To the degree that we have obeyed and followed the Spirit this has certainly been the result.

This does not mean that we do not have troubles or suffer attacks in which the enemy seeks to again impose his bondage and chaos in our lives. However, the Lord allows this to strengthen us and as we maintain our trust in Him we will always come out of them with even greater peace, harmony, and order in our life.

So basically we learn as we grow that a major way that we can distinguish between the work of God and the devil's schemes is by their fruit—one always resulting in order and peace, the other always seeking to bring disorder and fear.

Likewise, if we are living our lives so as to extend the Kingdom of God we should be leaving a trail of chaos and disorder transformed into order and peace. Just as the Holy Spirit moved upon the chaos in the beginning and brought forth such a wonderful creation with an order that is yet to be fathomed, He is never intimidated by chaos, but rather sees it as an opportunity. If we are led by the Spirit we will feel the same way. We will not be discouraged or distraught as we come across confusion or disorder, but rather see it as an opportunity to watch the Holy Spirit do a marvelous work.

THE ORDER OF THE CROSS

It is interesting that if you take the size of the tribes of Israel in the wilderness as stated in the Book of Numbers, and lay them out to scale in the order in which they were to march while in the wilderness, if you had looked down on them from above they were marching in the shape of a cross. When the Lord looked down on those He had redeemed from bondage He saw the cross. The cross is the basis that can alone bring about God's order into this world, and redeemed people can only march forward as they do so in and by the formation of the cross.

It is also noteworthy that if you were to draw a straight line through the furniture in the Tabernacle of Moses you would be drawing a cross. The Ark would be at the head of the cross and the brazen altar at its foot with the lampstand and table of shewbread being the arms. The head of Christ, which was once crowned with thorns, is now crowned with glory and honor—the Ark. The brazen altar, or the sacrifice, is now under His feet. We, in our journey into the glory of God, start at the foot of the cross and grow up into the head. This furniture was laid out as a step-by-step way to approach God, and there is no other way to approach Him except by the cross.

The brazen altar, where the sin offerings and other offerings were made for Israel, which was a foreshadowing of the sacrifice of Jesus on the cross, was the first object the people encountered as they passed through the door of the Outer Court. This is the first truth that we are confronted with after entering the door of faith and we must stop here and have our sins removed before we can proceed any further.

HANDLING THE WORD OF LIFE

In Exodus 27:3 we see that there were five different accessories that went with the altar's five different sacrifices, each of which represents an aspect of what the cross of Christ accomplished for us. The divine ordinances and laws governing the use of these instruments and the handling of the sacrifices on this altar were of extreme importance for the priests of the Lord to know and serve by. In First Samuel 2:12-17, we read of how the sons of Eli mishandled the sacrifices and they brought a curse upon themselves. The awesome, unfathomable responsibility of being entrusted with the gospel of the cross is not to be taken lightly. This is the greatest privilege that any creature in heaven or on the earth could ever be entrusted with.

GOD LIGHTS THE FIRE

In Leviticus 9:22-24 we are told that fire came out from the glory of the Lord to consume the sacrifice on the altar. In Leviticus 6:12-13 the priests are instructed to keep the fire on the altar "burning continually." By this we understand that the Lord must light the fire of the cross in a person's heart, but He expects us to keep it going. The cross is the one truth that we should never tire of, that we should never cease from proclaiming, and that we should never cease trying to understand its depths and glory. This is the one fire that must never go out in our life.

There is no worse condition that a Christian can fall into than lukewarmness. This is the ultimate deception. How could anyone who has truly encountered the living God, fathomed His grace, glory, and love, ever cease to be burning with passion to know Him better? What is more interesting in the universe than God? What is more wonderful than His fellowship? How could anyone who has beheld the love that He has for us—as demonstrated in His willingness to have done what He did—not marvel at Him daily? To become lukewarm about God could only happen to those who have fallen to the cares of this world or the delusion of idols.

THE CROSS—THE BASIS OF ALL LIGHT

It was the fire pans of this altar that were used to carry live coals from the altar to light the candlestick in the Holy

Place, and to burn incense on the golden altar of incense. By this we see that all of the light in the dwelling place of God originates at the cross. It is fire from this altar that was used to burn the incense, which represents our worship and intercession, because it is only by the fire of the cross in our lives that acceptable prayer and worship can originate. Just as it was the fire of the altar that lit every other fire in the Tabernacle, it is the fire of the cross that will light every other truth in our life.

The brazen altar was also large enough to fit all of the other pieces of furniture inside of it. This speaks of the fact that every other truth and blessing we receive from God is contained in the cross.

It is for this reason that we read in the Book of Revelation that after all things are concluded Jesus is still called "The Lamb." All of His truth, all of His gifts, power, and works, are wonderful and we should honor and be thankful for them, but let us never forget that all things are the result of the cross. The cross *carries* everything else and *lights* everything else. That is why, after all of the ministry all year long, when the priest went before the Ark, which represented the glory and presence of the Lord, he did not go without the blood.

It Is the Blood That Cleanses

Let us always remember that regardless of how much authority we have been entrusted with, how many miracles are done through us, even how many souls are saved through our preaching, we can only draw near to God because of the blood of Christ. We will never be able to approach on our own righteousness. Just as all of the articles of the Tabernacle had to be cleansed by the blood, Jesus' blood must cover our works or else they are not acceptable to be used in His presence—they are not clean.

Self-will is a desperate enemy of Christianity. The altar that we must come to is there for the taking of our self-life and self-will. Only when our self-will is fully dead can we fully know the will of God—the two are in conflict and cannot abide together:

> *And he who does not take up his cross and follow after Me is not worthy of Me. He who has found his life will lose it, and he who has lost his life for My sake will find it* (Matt. 10:38-39).

> *Whoever does not carry his own cross and come after Me cannot be My disciple* (Luke 14:27).

The altar was a place of blood and guts—it was not a pretty sight. Neither is the cross, but it is the power of God and the wisdom of God in its highest revelation. This is why Paul said:

> *For Christ did not send me to baptize, but to preach the gospel, not in cleverness of speech, so that the cross of Christ would not be made void. For the word of the cross is foolishness to those who are perishing, but to us who are being saved it is the power of God* (1 Cor. 1:17-18).

OUR GREATEST NEED

The greatest need in the Church today, and the very essence of the Kingdom of God, is the demonstration of God's power. We cannot be witnesses of the Almighty God without power. The power of God is also a revelation of His love because the power that He has bestowed on His Church is for healing and delivering those who are oppressed by the devil. The primary reason why there is so little power demonstrated in the Church has been our departure from the source of power—the cross. This is why the apostle Paul, one of the most learned men of his time, came to the following conclusion:

> *And when I came to you, brethren, I did not come with superiority of speech or of wisdom, proclaiming*

to you the testimony of God. For I determined to know nothing among you except Jesus Christ, and Him crucified. I was with you in weakness and in fear and in much trembling, and my message and my preaching were not in persuasive words of wisdom, but in demonstration of the Spirit and of power, so that your faith would not rest on the wisdom of men, but on the power of God....For the kingdom of God does not consist in words but in power (1 Corinthians 2:1-5; 4:20).

A basic spiritual principle revealed throughout the Scriptures is that power is released through sacrifice. This was demonstrated profoundly in the Passover sacrifice that set Israel free from Egypt. We can see in Second Kings 3:27 that this spiritual principle works for evil as well as good:

Then he [the king of Moab] *took his oldest son who was to reign in his place, and offered him as a burnt offering on the wall. And there came great wrath against Israel, and they departed from him and returned to their own land.*

Presently the satanic worshipers and cults seem to understand this more than most Christians. There is power in sacrifices, but if the power of this heathen king of Moab's sacrifice of his son could have such power, how much more power is released through the sacrifice of God's Son? There is no greater power in heaven or on earth than the cross.

⟪❦15❦⟫

Apostolic Sending

Today there is great interest in the apostolic ministry. Some believe that this ministry is essential to creating the order that the Church must come into, as discussed in the previous chapter. Others believe that it is creating much of the kind of confusion in the Church that we addressed in the chapters previous to that. In my travels and interchange with many different groups and movements within the Body of Christ, I would have to agree with both of these assessments. There seems to be a lot of good, and a lot of confusion coming out of the modern "apostolic" movements. I personally believe that this will continue to be the case, and will even increase, until true apostolic authority is restored to the Church, which I am personally still waiting for.

This does not mean that I do not believe that there are apostles today. I have believed this since I first became a Christian. I think some of those who are claiming to be apostles may really be. I think that it is also obvious that many who are making this claim do not measure up to the biblical stature of that ministry. Likewise, some of the teachings on the apostolic ministry that I have heard or read were very helpful, and some were woefully shallow at best and misleading at worst.

The questions of whether there are apostles today, and if so, defining who they are, are issues that the Church is obviously going to have to deal with. This chapter is by no means intended to answer all of the questions that have arisen from the modern apostolic movements or give definition to that ministry. Neither is it an attempt to bring correction to any one person or group.

I first taught this many years before it became the controversy that it now is. This is simply a teaching designed to clarify a few basic issues concerning this ministry to aid in missions and their fruitfulness. Because the foundation of any building will determine the strength of the whole building and likewise the strength of any mission—whether it is leading a mission to a nation or a people group, or starting a prayer meeting—the quality of the foundation will determine the fruitfulness, or lack of fruit, of the mission. Therefore this is a simple study of 12 basic principles of how the Lord Jesus sent out His apostles to their missions.

WHO IS SENDING?

The Greek word that is translated "apostle" in the New Testament basically means "one who is sent." The inference here is that apostles are ones who are sent by God. For this reason some have concluded that every missionary is an apostle, but that is not necessarily the case. All apostles are sent by God, but not everyone who is sent by God on a mission is an apostle, just as not everyone who preaches a sermon is a pastor.

There are also other biblical qualifications for the apostolic office that must be considered before we should attach the title "apostle" to a minister. However, because the very word *apostle* refers to the sending, how one is sent is an important factor that should be considered.

In Luke 10 we are given the most detailed outline of the way in which the Lord sends His messengers out. We also see in this text the kind of fruit that we can expect to see when one is sent out by the Lord, which is stated in verses 17-20:

The seventy returned with joy, saying, "Lord, even the demons are subject to us in Your name." And He said to them, "I was watching Satan fall from heaven like lightning. Behold, I have given you authority to tread upon serpents and scorpions, and over all the power of the enemy, and nothing will injure you. Nevertheless do not rejoice in this, that the spirits are subject to you, but rejoice that your names are recorded in heaven."

When the Lord sent out the 70, they experienced authority over demons, but there was actually something much greater taking place that they were not aware of—satan himself was being cast down from his place in the heavenly realm. This is the only place in Scripture that we are specifically shown how a principality in the heavenly realm is brought down. By this we must conclude that the ultimate form of spiritual warfare is apostolic sending.

We cast out demons, but we must "wrestle" with principalities and powers (Eph. 6:12 KJV). Wrestling is the closest form of combat. This is what true apostolic sending is for—going toe to toe with the powers of evil over the region that we are sent to. It is easy to understand why many would rather try to do this from their prayer closet, and certainly prayer is essential in all successful ministry. However, for a true victory over the devil's power over a region, there must be apostolic sending that results in an apostolic ministry that breaks the power of demonic strongholds.

Now let's back up and make a step-by-step study of just how the Lord sent out those whose ministry resulted in satan himself being cast down.

PRINCIPLE 1:

The first principle that we see in the way that the Lord sends out His messengers is in Luke 10:1, "Now after this the Lord appointed seventy others, and sent them in pairs...."

When the Lord sends His messengers out in the New Testament we consistently see them being sent in pairs. There are exceptions to this that we see in other ministries, such as with Philip the evangelist, but never with apostles. Even when apostles were sent to follow up on Philip's work in Samaria we see that two apostles were sent.

In the Old Testament we do often have prophets operating alone, but in the New Testament almost all ministry is done in teams, and all examples of apostolic work are done by teams of at least two. This is because one of the primary purposes of apostolic ministry is to build up the Church, which is supposed to be a Body of believers in which every member functions in harmony with the other parts of the Body. To do this, apostles must also be joined to the Body rightly, both demonstrating teamwork and imparting it as a basis for effective ministry.

We also know that spiritual authority is multiplied with unity, as we see in Leviticus 26:7-8, "But you will chase your enemies and they will fall before you by the sword; five of you will chase a hundred, and a hundred of you will chase ten thousand, and your enemies will fall before you by the sword." This is because unity requires humility and we know that "God is opposed to the proud, but gives grace to the humble" (James 4:6). We have no authority over the devil without God. To receive His grace requires that we be humble. Unity is a demonstration of this humility.

PRINCIPLE 2:

The next principle that we see concerning the way that the Lord sends out His messengers is that they were sent "...ahead of Him to every city and place where He Himself was going to come" (Luke 10:1). We only want to go where we know the Lord is going. Just as Moses prayed for the Lord not to send Israel anywhere unless His presence went with them, we must have the same devotion. Moses prayed this because he said that it was only by the Lord's presence with them that they could be distinguished from all of the other nations on the face of the earth (see Exod. 33:12-16). The same is true with us.

True Christianity is a restoration of the relationship between God and man that was lost by the fall. Our message is therefore not just in words, but in a demonstration of how this relationship has been restored. Our ministry should like-wise be a demonstration of our unity with the Lord by His presence being manifest with us.

We also know that we can do nothing without the Lord. Demons do not come out because they see us, but because they see the One who is with us. The Lord sent out the 70 to preach the Kingdom, and we have been sent for that same purpose. He sends His messengers of the Kingdom with the authority to demonstrate the power of His Kingdom. Jesus has authority over all of the power of the enemy, and He sends His messengers to demonstrate this. However, we only have true spiritual authority to the degree that the King abides in us. It is by His presence going with us that His work is accomplished through us.

PRINCIPLE 3:

The next principle is seen in Luke 10:2: "And He was saying to them, 'The harvest is plentiful, but the laborers are few; therefore beseech the Lord of the harvest to send out laborers into His harvest.' "

By this we see that even before we get going we need to start praying for reinforcements. One of the great tragedies of Christian missions has been our tendency to capture territory that we cannot hold. When the devil is cast out he will always try to get back in, as the Lord taught in Matthew 12:43-45. When evil spirits return and find their place unoc-cupied they not only come back, but will bring seven more demons that are even more wicked. By this the last state can be worse than the first. We must learn to go forth with a strategy for taking land and possessing it and occupying it.

There is often a conflict between those who are of the nature of spiritual pioneers and those who are more like settlers, wanting to occupy land to possess it and cultivate it. We desperately need both types in missions, and they need to learn to work together.

PRINCIPLE 4:

This we see in Luke 10:3, "Go; behold, I send you out as lambs in the midst of wolves." By this we see that we must be willing to go in the opposite spirit of those that we are being sent to. We must determine how a lamb should act in the place that we are called to, and how we can expect those to act who are still under the influence of the principality over the region.

For example, if the evil principality over a region is pride we will need to fortify ourselves constantly to walk in humility. If the evil over the region is greed we should resolve to be generous, etc. In this way we are to resolve to stand in the Holy Spirit counter to the evil in the place we are sent to, overcoming the evil with good.

I have been sent to live in a part of the country that has a spirit of poverty over it. It has amazed me how many good people come here and somehow fall to the delusion that they don't have to work for a living. I asked one man what he did for a living and he said, "I live by faith." I asked his wife what she did and she said, "I work so that he can live by faith!" It is interesting to me to see how much we need people in our area who believe in the prosperity aspects of the gospel, yet those all seem to live in the region that is controlled by the spirit of greed or selfish ambition, and their prosperity often (not always) seems to be a manifestation of pride rather than the biblical prosperity that is generosity.

The key to the success of any mission is to remain lambs even in the midst of wolves. Therefore a basic characteristic that all Christians must have who will accomplish their purpose is the ability to resist the pressure to conform. This is why Paul wrote in Galatians 1:10, "For am I now seeking the favor of men, or of God? Or am I striving to please men? If I were still trying to please men, I would not be a bond-servant of Christ."

One example of this principle that I experienced years ago was in the northeastern United States. I had a dream in which I was shone the principality over the region as a starving gray wolf. I immediately knew that this represented a spirit of pseudo-intellectualism (gray wolves in dreams and visions often speak of the brain—"gray matter"). The alarming part of the dream was that this wolf would have starved to death but it was being fed at the door of the church.

This dream caused me to expect to find church leadership there that was trying to reach their community with their brilliance and an intellectual approach to the gospel. That was precisely what I found. It was a sad state. Have you have ever witnessed how foolish someone comes across who tries to use words that are a little too big for them? That was the way that almost everyone I met came across. This tendency even came over the other speaker at the conference I was at. He began to attack the need for pursuing spiritual gifts and manifestations in place of understanding. I was shocked as this man had a reputation for being a great Pentecostal/Charismatic teacher who supposedly moved in a lot of power.

The Church does have the authority to loose in heaven and have it loosed on the earth. I left convinced that the pseudo-intellectual spirit over that region actually was being fed, and probably even kept alive, by the Church there. I was likewise convinced that the people of that region would especially respond to the gifts of the Spirit and power, but the atmosphere of doubt created in the conference that I was in made it very difficult to even teach on such things, much less begin to move in them. Remember that even the Lord could not do many miracles when there was such an atmosphere of unbelief (see Matt. 13:58).

This principle is probably a reason why the Lord sent Paul to the Gentiles and Peter to the Jews. Both were sent to those that they would actually be offensive to. This compelled both of them to have to rely on the Holy Spirit if they were to be successful in their ministry.

PRINCIPLE 5:

This is found in Luke 10:4, "Carry no money belt, no bag, no shoes...." This implies that there must be a basic dependence on the provision of the Lord for His missions.

I personally violated this principle once to the point of offending the Lord. I did it by starting a business with the motivation of making enough money so that I would fully support myself in ministry. That may seem noble, but not when doing it out of pride like I was. I wanted to get to the place where I would never even need to take up an offering. I justified this by saying that I wanted to keep my motives free from seeking financial reward for any ministry, and that was partly true, but I also hated asking people for support.

I attained the net worth that was my goal in just a few years and was ready to start turning over my business to others so that I could return to the full-time ministry. I then had an encounter with the Lord in which He let me know how offended He was by this. He said simply, "Do you not think that I can provide for My own ministry?"

The Lord then asked me to give my business to Him. (I noted that He did not say that it was His business.) He then quickly consumed the business and my net worth was reduced to zero. I lost everything that I had worked so hard for, but I felt more free and was happier than I had been in all of the years that I was in business. He also immediately began to provide for me and our ministry far more abundantly than I could have ever dreamed.

I do believe that the Lord blesses some people so that they can support the work of the Kingdom, but watch out for the trap of trying to manipulate the Lord into blessing us so that we can give to His work. That can be very offensive to Him, inferring that He cannot do it.

PRINCIPLE 6:

This one is found in the last part of Luke 10:4: "and greet no one on the way." Why doesn't the Lord want us to greet anyone while we are on the way to our mission? If you live in the South you are used to greeting everyone you pass whether you know them or not, but in most of the world you would only greet close friends or relatives. The principle here is that if we are going to be distracted from our mission it is likely to come from our friends or relatives.

PRINCIPLE 7:

The next principle is found in Luke 10:5-6, "Whatever house you enter, first say, 'Peace be to this house.' If a man of peace is there, your peace will rest upon him; but if not, it will return to you." Walking in the peace of God is crucial to walking in His presence. This is why He chose Jerusalem to be His dwelling place—Jerusalem means "city of peace." We will know where the Lord is dwelling by His peace.

PRINCIPLE 8:

The next principle is in Luke 10:7: "Stay in that house, eating and drinking what they give you; for the laborer is worthy of his wages." There will always be some who perceive the ministry to be a place to personally prosper, being motivated by selfish ambition. Moneychangers still tend to flock to the temple. However, those who are truly sent by God will be of a different character. It is usually more difficult for them to receive than to give. They will often have skills whereby they could earn much more in a secular profession, and yet they will still have a hard time receiving from the resources that are devoted to the spreading of the gospel. This is an exhortation from the Lord to understand that His laborers are worthy of their wages and they should receive them without guilt.

It is important for ministers of the gospel to receive their provision from those that you are sent to because teaching the people to be generous givers is essential for having the Lord dwell among us. That is why Moses built the Tabernacle of God from the freewill offering of the people. In this age the Lord will only dwell where He is wanted. We see in Revelation 3 that He will even stand outside of His own Church and knock in order to be let in. Those who are not willing to sacrifice their stuff so that the Lord can dwell among them are certainly not worthy of Him.

PRINCIPLE 9:

The next principle is in verse 7, "Do not keep moving from house to house." Those who are sent by God to a city or region should let the peace of God lead them to the right door, and then we must resist being a spiritual opportunist, but stay with those who open the door for us as long as the peace of God is there. Those who are the first to open their doors to a messenger from God will inevitably be the ones with the greatest faith.

PRINCIPLE 10:

The next principle is in Luke 10:8: "Whatever city you enter and they receive you, eat what is set before you." This is an exhortation not to resist hospitality, and not to offend people's local customs.

PRINCIPLE 11:

The next principle is in Luke 10:9: "and heal those in it who are sick, and say to them, 'The kingdom of God has come near to you.' " Some versions say "heal and proclaim." This is a statement about how the healing ministry is united with the proclamation of the Kingdom. Everywhere that the Lord went He healed the sick, and as He said in John 17:18, "As You sent Me into the world, I also have sent them into the world."

Sickness is a result of the fall. This does not necessarily mean that any time we get sick it is because we sinned. Often sickness is simply an attack from the devil. Even so, the most basic message of the Kingdom is the redemption from the fall and the reversal of its consequences. There are few things that demonstrate this greater than healing the sick, which is evidence of the Kingdom of God being near.

The high priest under the Levitical priesthood had bells and pomegranates sown alternately around the hem of his garments. Pomegranates were used in ancient times for medicine, and they usually represent healing in Scripture. Bells represent proclamations or messages. Every time the high priest would move, the pomegranates would strike the bells and their sound would go forth. This was a prophetic picture of how every time Jesus the High Priest moved, the message of healing would go forth. This is still true.

It is also noteworthy that the woman who had the issue of blood that could not be cured touched the hem of the Lord's garments and was healed. Many believe that she did this in recognition of how the hem of the high priest's garments represented healing, and that Jesus was the true High Priest.

PRINCIPLE 12:

For this one let's again read Luke 10:17-20:

The seventy returned with joy, saying, "Lord, even the demons are subject to us in Your name." And He said to them, "I was watching Satan fall from heaven like lightning. Behold, I have given you authority to tread upon serpents and scorpions, and over all the power of the enemy, and nothing will injure you. Nevertheless do not rejoice in this, that the spirits are subject to you, but rejoice that your names are recorded in heaven."

When we are sent by the Lord, we will have authority over all of the power of the enemy. Because of this we need to ask another obvious question: How many are walking in this authority? I do not know of anyone, which leads us to another obvious question: Why? As this text indicates, we should be constantly ambushing the enemy and attacking him rather than constantly being subject to his schemes.

SUMMARY

One primary reason why we are not walking in the full authority that we have been given over the enemy and over disease is directly related to how we are sent. This is not to imply that we are not doing anything right, or are not being sent by God on our missions, since obviously we do have some authority over the devil and some authority over disease. The Lord is blessing our work as much as He can. However, we can conclude that a reason we are not having true apostolic results is that we do not yet have true apostolic sending.

We can be encouraged that there is so much emphasis today on the need for apostolic ministry. In perceiving this need many may have run ahead a bit, calling many things apostolic that do not quite measure up to the biblical stature of that ministry. It seems to have been for this same reason that the Lord commended the Ephesian Church in Revelation 2:2 because they "put to the test those who call themselves apostles, and they are not, and you found them to be false."

Because much of what is today being called apostolic obviously does not measure up to the true apostolic, it is turning many away from anything or anyone who claims apostolic authority. That may be expected, but it is not the remedy. We need to continue seeking the Lord for the true apostolic message to go forth with true apostolic authority.

There is more to this issue than can be covered in a single chapter such as this. Even so, it is essential that we search them out, and seek the restoration of true apostolic authority that will result in a true apostolic Church being raised up again. The Scripture is clear that we can expect this before the end of the age comes, and regardless of how muddied these waters may seem to get at times from men trampling in them, we can be sure that a pure flow will come.

Whether we personally attain to full apostolic authority or not we must continue to pursue all of the authority that the Lord intended for His Church to have, and recover as much as we can for those who may come after us. The pursuit of the apostolic is a noble and important pursuit, but by the very nature of the word *apostle* it has to begin with how and by whom we are sent.

For another important insight on this we should proceed down a few verses to Luke 10:21:

> *At that very time He rejoiced greatly in the Holy Spirit, and said, "I praise You, O Father, Lord of heaven and earth, that You have hidden these things from the wise and intelligent and have revealed them to infants. Yes, Father, for this way was well-pleasing in Your sight."*

The Greek word that is translated "praise" in this verse is *agalliao*, which is defined as "to jump for joy, to exult, to be exceedingly glad, with exceeding joy, to rejoice greatly." The verse quoted above was much more than the Lord just quietly offering a nice prayer of thanks to His Father. The word He used that is translated as "praise" indicates that He was jumping for joy at the fact that the Father had hidden the secrets of His Kingdom from the wise and intelligent and revealed them to babes, or we might say, "the immature."

Why would this thing cause so much joy in the Lord? This is obviously related to what He said Matthew 18:23: "And He called a child to Himself and set him before them, and said, 'Truly I say to you, unless you are converted and become like children, you will not enter the kingdom of heaven." Why is this? What is the quality that a child has that we must have to enter the Kingdom? Probably the most important is humility, which the Lord emphasized in the next verse, "Whoever then humbles himself as this child, he is the greatest in the kingdom of heaven" (Matt. 18:4).

Pride is what caused the first fall, the fall of lucifer, and has been a chief factor in every fall since. Therefore the basic characteristic of those who would enter the Kingdom of God, reversing the fall, is for us to humble ourselves before the Lord. One of the primary characteristics of the humble, which is also a primary characteristic of children, is that they are teachable.

It is because we are still in our pride that we come up with many exalted ideals about what an apostle should be like, when the Lord sends those who are the very ones that pride will cause us to overlook. Consider this description of the greatest apostles that the world has yet seen from First Corinthians 4:9-13:

> *For, I think, God has exhibited us apostles last of all, as men condemned to death; because we have become a spectacle to the world, both to angels and to men. We are fools for Christ's sake, but you are prudent in Christ; we are weak, but you are strong; you are distinguished, but we are without honor. To this present hour we are both hungry and thirsty, and are poorly clothed, and are roughly treated, and are homeless; and we toil, working with our own hands; when we are reviled, we bless; when we are persecuted, we endure; when we are slandered, we*

try to conciliate; we have become as the scum of the world, the dregs of all things, even until now.

How many of us now want the job? Why would the Lord of glory send His own messengers in such a humble state? Why would He Himself come as a lowly carpenter from the lowliest town in the lowliest nation on earth at the time? Why doesn't He reveal His glory and power to the world through the most magnificent angels, displaying them for all to see, and then all would bow their knee to Him. Because the gateway into His Kingdom is humility.

As long as we continue trying to reach the world with our greatness we will fall short of the true apostolic. Were not the greatest miracles always the result of the greatest needs? We all seem to want great miracles, but no one seems willing to be put in the place where they will need them. Possibly the main reason why we don't have many true apostles is that we are not yet willing to become low enough, needy enough, to look foolish enough, or to be persecuted enough, to be apostles. As we read in First Corinthians 1:26-29:

> *For consider your calling, brethren, that there were not many wise according to the flesh, not many mighty, not many noble; but God has chosen the foolish things of the world to shame the wise, and God has chosen the weak things of the world to shame the things which are strong, and the base things of the world and the despised God has chosen, the things that are not, so that He may nullify the things that are, so that no man may boast before God.*

We should note here that the apostle did not say that the Lord did not call *any* noble, wise, etc., but rather not many. Paul himself was from among the nobility and was possibly one of the most learned men of his times. However, Paul said that he counted anything that he was in the flesh as dung compared to the simple knowledge of Christ. He was willing to become poor, despised, and persecuted for the sake of the gospel he carried. He even acknowledged to the Corinthians that he came in "weakness and in fear and in much trembling..." (1 Cor. 2:3). He acknowledged to the Galatians that his flesh had been a "trial" to them (Gal. 4:14). How many of us would even invite someone like that to speak in our church? It was a message and a messenger that required everyone who received it to humble themselves and be teachable. That is the nature of the true apostolic. Do we still want it?

For the true apostles the answer to this question will be yes. They are more than willing to be viewed as the scum of this earth to fulfill their purpose in the Lord. For them this is not about ego or personal fulfillment. They died to those when they were called. The true apostolic call is the call to die, so that He might live His life through us. When ministries are built upon a foundation of that kind of death, the death of the cross, we will also see through them the power of the resurrection life of Jesus as well.

OTHER TITLES IN THE SERIES

BREAKING THE POWER OF EVIL
ISBN 0-7684-2163-2

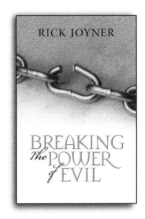

The gates of hell are the entrances through which evil gains access to the world. Rick Joyner, author of the best-selling book *The Final Quest*, dramatically exposes the insidious cruelty of evil as manifested in jealousy, fear, spirit of poverty, spiritual authority, and religious spirits.

Breaking the Power of Evil equips the Church with the tools necessary to first create a barrier into our world, and second, open a door into the heavenly realm. Joyner announces that the battle is one of territory—and one that is a struggle for the human heart. It is in the heart where evil must be broken. With prophetic precision, Joyner carefully casts a prophetic light that will dispel the darkness as it enlightens the soul.

OVERCOMING EVIL IN THE LAST DAYS
ISBN 0-7684-2178-0

As the gates of hell unleash their fiendish fury against the souls of man, the church must rise up and stand against them. There is a time to stand up and turn the other cheek and there is a time to stand. Now is the time to stand.

Joyner lifts the veil on this horde exposing the hideous face of racism, witchcraft and religious spirits. The challenge is clear. We must maintain our warrior stance against evil as we persist in our primary calling—worshiping and loving God.

AUTHOR CONTACT INFORMATION

For information about the ministry of Rick Joyner and other books and materials that are available by him, you can call

1-800-542-0278

for a free catalog or visit the website at

www.morningstarministries.org.

Available at your local Christian bookstore.

For more information and sample chapters, visit www.destinyimage.com

Additional copies of this book and other
book titles from DESTINY IMAGE are
available at your local bookstore.

For a bookstore near you, call 1-800-722-6774

Send a request for a catalog to:

Destiny Image® Publishers, Inc.
P.O. Box 310
Shippensburg, PA 17257-0310

*"Speaking to the Purposes of God for This
Generation and for the Generations to Come"*

**For a complete list of our titles,
visit us at www.destinyimage.com**